Speak to Me, Lord, I'm Listening

BETSY TACCHELLA

InspiringVoices®

A Service of **Guideposts**

Scripture quotations taken from the New American Standard Bible®, Copyright © 1960, 1962, 1963, 1968, 1971, 1972, 1973, 1975, 1977, 1995 by The Lockman Foundation. Used by permission." (www.Lockman.org)

Revised Standard Version of the Bible, copyright 1952 [2nd edition, 1971] by the Division of Christian Education of the National Council of the Churches of Christ in the United States of America. Used by permission. All rights reserved.

Scripture taken from the King James Version of the Bible.

Scriptures taken from the Holy Bible, New International Version®, NIV®. Copyright © 1973, 1978, 1984, 2011 by Biblica, Inc.™ Used by permission of Zondervan. All rights reserved worldwide. www.zondervan.com The "NIV" and "New International Version" are trademarks registered in the United States Patent and Trademark Office by Biblica, Inc.™ All rights reserved.

Inspiring Voices books may be ordered through booksellers or by contacting:

Inspiring Voices
1663 Liberty Drive
Bloomington, IN 47403
www.inspiringvoices.com
1 (866) 697-5313

Because of the dynamic nature of the Internet, any web addresses or links contained in this book may have changed since publication and may no longer be valid. The views expressed in this work are solely those of the author and do not necessarily reflect the views of the publisher, and the publisher hereby disclaims any responsibility for them.

Any people depicted in stock imagery provided by Thinkstock are models, and such images are being used for illustrative purposes only. Certain stock imagery © Thinkstock.

ISBN: 978-1-4624-0976-1 (sc)
ISBN: 978-1-4624-0977-8 (e)

Library of Congress Control Number: 2014909238

Printed in the United States of America.

Inspiring Voices rev. date: 06/05/2014

Contents

"Thus says the Lord, the God of Israel, 'write all the words which I have spoken to you in a book'" (Jer. 30:2).

Preface

YOU MAY BE wondering where my book title came from and why there is an umbrella before each chapter. The title of my book, "Speak to Me, Lord, I'm Listening," is taken from an encounter Samuel had with the Lord in I Samuel 3:10. Samuel, a young boy living with Eli, the priest, was asleep in bed when he was awakened by a voice speaking to him. Assuming it was Eli, he arose and went to see what he wanted. Eli said it wasn't him who spoke and sent Samuel back to bed. The call came again, and again, Eli sent him back to bed. On the third time, Eli realized it was the Lord calling Samuel. A word from the Lord was rare in those days (I Sam. 3:1) but He had chosen at this time to speak to Samuel. *Then the Lord came and stood and called as at other times, "Samuel! Samuel!" And Samuel said, "Speak, for your servant is listening"* (1Sam. 3:10).

It is striking that Samuel quickly answered in such a humble fashion, *"Speak, for your servant is listening."* He was ready to listen and observe whatever the Lord spoke to him. In the same way, this book is an opportunity to renew our understanding that God still speaks to people today, that He is still looking for people who will listen and respond. Thus, the title, "Speak to Me, Lord, I'm Listening," is a call for us to also be attentive to God's voice in our day.

You may also be wondering what an umbrella at the beginning of each chapter could possibly have to do with hearing God's voice. Symbolically, it will play an important role but you will not realize its significance until you finish reading the book. So, enjoy the stories as they build to a culmination of insight regarding the umbrella's significance. And thank you for reading my book. May the journey bless you.

CHAPTER 1

Listen and Hear My Voice

*"Give ear and hear my voice, listen
and hear my words" (Isa. 28:23).*

I ONCE ASKED A friend if she had ever heard God's voice. Without blinking, her quick reply was, "No, I don't think I ever have, have you?" Her answer took me by surprise at first. After talking with her further, I realized the problem was not that she had never heard God's voice but that she was not aware when He was speaking to her.

As we continued our conversation, I asked her about some situations in her life and their outcomes. We talked about how God speaks in many different ways, through the Bible, prayer, circumstances, at times through His creation, friends, books, a sermon, a dream and sometimes, through life's lessons.

It was fun to experience with her the joy of realizing there had been many situations in her life when God had indeed spoken to her. Her eyes were opened to the possibility that hearing His voice was a significant element in her relationship with Him. I hoped she would begin to watch for these times, recognize them, and even count them as important signs that God had faith adventures in store for her.

Expecting to hear God's voice adds excitement and delight to our faith journey with Him.

Perhaps, at times, we all need this aspect of our walk with Christ polished a bit. Come along with me as I share times when I was aware God was speaking to me. As you read my experiences, I hope they will touch something in your heart and bring to your remembrance similar times when God has also spoken a personal word to you. Like me, I think you will find an increase in your joy and a sense of expectation as you anticipate gaining insight about God through hearing his voice. Proverbs 8:6 encourages us with these words, *"Listen, for I will speak noble things; and the opening of my lips will reveal right things."*

This first story is one where God caught my attention in an unusual way. Sometimes, God teaches us through events He allows in our lives. Watch for the message He revealed to me. You may not have endured the same kind of incident but you probably have your own experiences of a lesson learned and truth revealed.

Tested by Fire

Our beautiful, newly built home stood nestled among the rolling hills of Northern California. Golden grasses waved in the breeze, hardy oak trees majestically dotted the landscape, and a quiet creek trickled in the ravine below. Our eyes feasted on the beauty around us. Because of designated open land behind our home, we were surrounded by acres of open space and could have walked a great distance without encountering another home.

It was moving day. While my husband, Bill, and our older daughter, Kim, ran some errands, our ten year old daughter, Laurie, and I confronted the task of unpacking. Moving from box to box in a second floor bedroom, arranging and rearranging, we enjoyed light conversation and the fun of settling into our new home. How fleeting was this tranquil moment. As Laurie walked across the room to unpack the next box, a flash of something outside caught her attention. Immediately transfixed, with a startled look on her face, she stood gazing out the bedroom window trying to make sense of what she was seeing.

"Mommy," she cried out, her voice tight with alarm and fear, not believing what she was seeing. "The hill behind our house is on fire!"

Sure it is, I thought nonchalantly, her words not registering in my preoccupied mind. To appease her, I pulled myself up from the scattered boxes and packing paper and peered out the window myself. Immediate panic seized my heart as I stood riveted on the roaring flames. I watched as they devoured the dry, three foot high golden grasses close to our home. Stunned, I attempted to process the raging fire eating its way down the hill toward our home. Standing transfixed, for a moment I couldn't move.

Shaken with fear, anxious thoughts began to grip me. *What would happen to our beautiful, new home? What would happen to us, to our dreams?* Laurie and I quickly ran down the stairs to call the fire department. Wait! We didn't have phone service yet! (Cell phones were a decade away from being invented). Hands trembling, I grabbed my car keys. "Hurry Laurie, we have to go for help." Literally lunging into the car, we sped to a friend's house. Would we contact the fire department in time?

How quickly I had forgotten that the previous night we had gathered with some close friends to dedicate our new home to the Lord. We knew this house was a gift from Him. When we had looked for a lot to build on, this one surrounded by acres of rolling hills was our first choice. But a sale was pending with many others on a waiting list. It seemed there wasn't even a remote possibility that we could have this site.

We had prayed that somehow that lot could be ours, but it didn't look hopeful. Then one evening, as Bill and I played tennis at our community tennis courts, our realtor, whose office was across the street, dashed out of his workplace and sprinted toward us waving papers and calling out, "It's yours if you still want it!" Through an unusual set of circumstances, our name, which had been about 80th on the list, had reached the top of the list. Now, would we lose our dream house in a fire?

Parking in our friend Bev's driveway, I burst into her family room screaming hysterically, "I have to call the fire department. Our house is in the path of a grass fire!" Fumbling with fear, I misdialed twice.

Busy! The fire department line was busy! How is that possible? After what seemed an endless time of dialing and redialing, help was on the way.

"Pray God will change the wind to blow away from any homes," I frantically cried out to Bev as we made a dash for the car. As we drove, Laurie and I fervently prayed that God would intervene and spare our house.

By now, neighbors had seen the flames spreading and had gathered to help. Scaffolding left by the builders served as a ladder to the roof where they hosed the shingles. Bill soon arrived home. He and others sprinted up the hill behind our house with sickles and shovels ready to cut down the tall grass and dig trenches in an effort to stop the fire.

Clinging to a friend in the driveway, we cried out to God to redirect the fire to go up the hill where there were no homes. After some minutes, I raised my tear soaked eyes to assess the situation. Looking around, I observed that it appeared the fire had begun to move in a different direction. Blinking several times to see more clearly, yes, there was a change taking place in the wind pattern. Where it had previously curled up over the hill blowing smoke and flames straight for our house, it now appeared to be moving in the opposite direction. Was it possible that God, in an amazing turn of events, had pursued the winds and commanded them to turn away in answer to our prayers?

With a shift in the wind, the crisis began to wane and the fire came under control. Several firemen remained on the hill all night watching for renewed sparks on the seventy burned acres. Their muted conversation quietly drifted down the hill all through the evening hours. The thick smell of smoke permeated the air and wafted throughout the house. As the hours passed, I pondered the awesomeness of God in contrast to my delirious response to this situation. Ever so softly, God began to speak to me about the events of the day. It was somewhat like a dialogue between two friends. In His gentle way, He led my thinking first to a review of what had happened. As I pondered the events of the day, including my overreaction and panic, I sensed God ever so gently begin to speak to my heart. He helped me to acknowledge that my reactions were completely void of faith. Then He reminded me of one word which aptly described who He was in the situation.

That word was *faithful.* It was as if He said to me that, in the midst of my unfaithfulness, He is always faithful. Through that one word, He taught me a powerful lesson. I sensed God's love, His compassion, and His presence surrounding me. His mercy was as thick in the air as the smoke that continued to waft into the house. In the midst of this peaceful time of reflection, I made a decision that the next time we had a crisis, I would choose faith. I didn't have to wait long.

Retested by Mud

After a wonderful year and a half in our dream home, a job transfer called us to another move. With the "For Sale" sign properly placed in the yard, we left for the afternoon while the realtor had an open house. Though it was an overcast rainy day, we felt confident we would soon see a "Sold" sign in the yard. After all, scores of people had wanted this lot before we got it.

As we arrived home that dark, rainy evening, a nervous, pacing realtor met us in the driveway. "You'll never guess what happened!" he anxiously exclaimed. Confident he was about to tell us he had sold the house, we prodded him on. "Well," he began, still pacing and obviously agitated, "I was showing the house to a couple when someone called down from upstairs, 'Have you ever had problems with mud slides in this area?' Laughing, I assured her we had not."

"Oh, my!" she yelled as she peered out the window. "You do now!" At that moment a huge section of earth slid down into our back yard. Fortunately, the now half toppled wood fence kept it from oozing closer to the house.

We grabbed a flashlight and headed out back. Sure enough, there it was, a twenty foot wide gaping breach in the hill and tons of mud pressing against our fence, slowly seeping into the back yard. It reminded us of a calving glacier where a section of the side of a glacier collapses and flows into the sea.

My immediate response almost surprised me. I laughed! Instantly, I recalled the fire and how God had been faithful even when I had faltered. I could almost hear God laughing with me.

Seeing the mud slide, my faith soared. What a challenge to trust Him! Reason and intellect told me that it would be impossible to sell this house now. Someone would have to be crazy to buy a house with a sliding hill and no guarantee the mud wouldn't be in the house with the next rain.

I sensed God cheering me on with this personal word of reminder. *Remember the fire, Betsy? Remember how I was faithful? I'm pleased with your decision not to react to the mud. Watch what I'm about to do next.*

In my mind, I had the distinct impression that God was having fun, that He had something up His sleeve that would bless us. He absolutely loves what we call impossible situations, times when we are out of resources, occasions when we can't fix a problem.

Lord, I prayed, *we know you have called us to move. You have just made it perfectly clear again that this is Your house, and I believe you will take care of selling it. I trust you to step in and take over. Thank you.* We knew at that moment that if this house sold, it would clearly be God's doing. We were reminded of the words in Mark 10:27 where Jesus said, *"With people it is impossible, but not with God; for all things are possible with God."*

The next day we looked out the window at the still oozing mud slide. I was at peace and still smiling. Even with some city clean up, the hole in the hill remained obvious. There was no mistake about what had happened. We continued to pray each day, *Thank you, Lord, that you are bigger than a mud slide. We rely on you for the sale of this house.*

Within one week we had two offers and sold the house for our asking price. God had truly worked another miracle. But I wonder which was the greater miracle, that He sold a house with a mud slide, or that He spoke through two complicated situations, changing my heart from panic to peace, from little faith to trust in the Lord.

Reflection

Although God did not speak to me with audible words in the circumstance of the fire and mud, His tenderness toward me eased my mind so that I could hear and receive a clear and important message. With no condemnation, I felt loved and cared for as God simply reminded me that He is faithful. With just that simple word and the demonstration of it, my faith rose and my trust was secured.

Have you ever encountered a situation where somehow you came out on the other side having learned a powerful life lesson? Could that be God using a circumstance to speak into your life? Could that be God revealing something important to you? The bigger questions in any trial are these: What is God trying to reveal to me? What response is He looking for? Did I cooperate and learn the valuable lesson He is trying to teach me?

With this as criteria, God unmistakably spoke to me as I processed the fire. He showed me that He chose to spare our house and how all of my anxiety and fear were useless in that situation. He had a bigger plan unfolding and used the fire to challenge me in regard to His faithfulness. My response in the end was to accept that He can be trusted to be faithful.

When the mud came, my confidence in Him was strong, strong enough to laugh at the situation. I had history with God. I knew He would have a plan. Many life lessons come from situations we experience. God uses each of these as a teaching tool. What is He looking for? Possibly a change of heart and a renewed mind to trust Him.

Trials in life have the potential for God to produce good things in us. He has purpose in the trials we experience. James 1:3-4 explains that He uses difficulties to produce endurance. Romans 5:3-5 adds that tribulation produces perseverance, character, and hope.

When we look at a lake that is perfectly smooth, we often say it's as smooth as glass. Why is it smooth? Because there are no waves causing turbulence or upheaval. The water is at peace. Interestingly, God revealed to me that it's also possible to be at peace in the midst of a fiery experience. In my case, fire and turmoil led to mud and peace - all because God chose to speak into my circumstance as I processed my responses. He was and is faithful.

Tune in to His Voice

Does God speak to His people today? Emphatically, yes! Isaiah 28:23 says it well. *"Give ear and hear my voice, listen and hear my words."* A logical question might be this, "Why would the Lord exhort us to hear His voice and listen to His words if He didn't plan to speak to us?" Truly, His creativity in communicating knows no bounds or limits.

A pastor once said, "Wouldn't it seem practical that when we meet with God that He might have something to say?" In our time with the Lord, do we allow moments for listening? Prayer is so much more than just us talking; it's an exciting give and take relationship with both parties contributing to the conversation.

Think of a close friendship in your life. Perhaps you will agree that one of the joys of friendship is the exchange as you dialogue back and forth. What if one of you did all the talking and never gave room for any response? Would that really qualify as a personal relationship? It's the same with God. He loves hearing us converse with Him. Our praise, worship, petitions, and just telling him how we're feeling are so valuable to God that He receives our prayers in golden bowls. Revelation 5:8 calls them *"golden bowls full of incense, which are the prayers of the saints."* Yet, do we consider His response to us as equally precious and worthy?

Is it possible that listening in prayer might even be more important than speaking? James 1:19 says, *"This you know, my beloved brethren.*

But everyone must be quick to hear, slow to speak and slow to anger." And Ecclesiastes 5:12 gives a reminder to *"Guard your steps as you go to the house of God, and draw near to <u>listen</u>..."*

To Israel or Not

When our oldest daughter, Kim, attended Taylor University, she planned to join a group from her college on a four week tour of Israel. As is often the case in Israel, reports of uprisings in that part of the world were prevalent. Some considered it a dangerous place to travel. Machine gun laden soldiers were frequently seen by tourists. Due to the unrest, many concerned travelers opted to change their plans.

Upon hearing news reports, Kim's grandparents expressed concern about her trip. We also felt some apprehension. Bill and I decided to commit the matter to prayer and trust God to speak to us on Kim's behalf. *Lord, Kim is planning a trip to Israel. We're a little uneasy about the situation over there. Would you give us a verse of Scripture that would provide direction and settle our hearts?*

That day, as I did my Bible reading, the issue of Kim's travel weighed on me. As I turned the page, a verse from Psalm 125 caught my attention, *"As the mountains surround Jerusalem, so the Lord surrounds His people from this time forth and forever"* (Ps. 125:2).

These words seemed to leap from the page. I have grown to recognize that when that happens, it is often God speaking to me. The words from the Psalm felt so personal. They stirred my heart and even brought a sense of confirmation and peace. I had expected to hear God's voice, and I was not disappointed. I pictured the Lord tenderly surrounding Kim with His hand of protection throughout her trip. We knew we could trust Him and felt reassured that He would keep her safe in Israel. Relying on this Scripture as a personal word from the Lord, we confidently released her to go.

A word from God is often straightforward, uncomplicated, and concise. It brings peace, knowledge, and perspective. Confirmation through a verse of Scripture in this case enabled us to lay aside fretting and worry about Kim's safety and replace it with faith. In retrospect, the trip went well. She had a wonderful three weeks and was never in any real danger.

The Scriptures tell us that we are to enter into God's rest. Ability to rest in the Lord comes when we are reassured that He is in control. Because He loves us so much, He is willing to speak words of comfort and assurance. Our part is to listen and heed. How often do we stew, brood, and strive over a situation because we don't see it from God's viewpoint and thereby miss the confidence that comes from receiving a word from the Lord? At times, we desperately need to hear from God. It's the only road to tranquility, a calm spirit, and quietness of soul.

What Does the Bible Say?

Let's look at some verses that confirm that it is biblical to hear God's voice. We will see that it is, in fact, God's desire to speak to His children. John 10:27 says, *"My sheep hear My voice and I know them and they follow Me."*

After I became a Christian, the truth of that verse impacted me. Thinking back I remembered countless times when I had heard God's voice. At the time, I had not realized that He was speaking to me because I had never considered the idea of hearing His voice. The Word says His sheep hear His voice. Therefore, by faith, we can be sure that it is possible to hear from God.

Rhema Word

John 8:47 declares, *"He who is of God hears the words of God...."* This means that when we belong to God, we are in a position to hear His words. This verse uses the idea of words in an interesting way. Let's look at the meaning of *"word"* in Greek.

In the Greek language, there are two commonly used words that mean *"word."* The first is logos, and it includes the entire written Word of God, both Old and New Testaments. It has a general meaning and includes all Scripture. When you sit down and read your Bible, you are reading the logos word. Through the logos word, God reveals Himself to man in written words.

Rhema, a second Greek term which also means *"word,"* has a more specific meaning. Used seventy times in the New Testament, it refers to a specific word from God which He speaks in a personal way to an individual in a particular situation. It's a message from the heart of God that speaks directly to a situation at hand. Whereas logos encompasses a broad view of the entire written word of God, rhema is a narrow personal word appropriate to a present need or circumstance.

When I received the verse of assurance of Kim's safety as she prepared to travel to an endangered part of the world, it was a rhema word. The Holy Spirit quickened a verse of (logos) Scripture to my spirit so that I knew God had spoken to me (rhema). Without this personal word from the Lord regarding her specific situation, we would have hesitated allowing her to go to Israel and would have certainly experienced a measure of anxiety.

Of course, it is important to remember that any rhema word from God must align itself with the logos word. If we think we have received a word from God and it is in opposition to the revealed logos word, then we should pause to consider its source. We will address this more later.

Hearing a rhema word from the logos Scripture is one way to acknowledge God's voice. However, there are other ways. Listen to Bill's conversation with his friend.

Conversation with a Friend

Although Scripture is one way to receive a word from God, we cannot limit Him to that as the only way. Does that mean that God can speak to people other than through the Bible?

While visiting with a friend we'll call Ken, Bill and he launched into a conversation concerning this issue. "Bill, my understanding is that God only speaks through His written Word, the Bible."

"I guess I see it differently," Bill said, "but I can understand how many Christians see it that way. Through Biblical examples and my own experience, it seems there are many times God speaks to people by means other than Scripture."

"Give me an example," Ken pursued with peaked but skeptical interest.

Bill continued. "I see in Scripture that God sometimes spoke to people directly or through another person, a circumstance, or by whatever means He chose. Let's look at Paul's experience in Acts 13:2-4. *While they were ministering to the Lord and fasting, the Holy Spirit said, 'Set apart for Me Barnabas and Saul for the work to which I have called them.' Then, when they had fasted and prayed and laid their hands on them, they sent them away. So, being sent out by the Holy Spirit, they went down to Seleucia and from there they sailed to Cyprus.*"

"Do you notice that the disciples were ministering to the Lord and fasting when the Holy Spirit said, '*Set apart for Me Barnabas and Saul for the work to which I have called them.*' This directive from the Holy Spirit was the word that sent them on their first missionary journey. This rhema word, directly from the Holy Spirit, convinced Paul and Barnabas to move into action.

"We don't know exactly how this word came to them, but it was powerful enough for these godly men to change their direction. I think there are many questions in life that are not directly addressed in Scripture, Ken. Which girl should I marry? Should I take this job or that one? Should we buy this house? Should we move at all? These are big questions, but I can't think of a verse that gives me a specific answer. However, there are Scriptures that guide us, teach us principles and character, give us vision, and help us count the cost as we make decisions. Are you seeing, Ken, that every question is not answered specifically in the Bible?"

Bill then asked Ken, "Looking back at Paul's encounter with the Holy Spirit in Acts, where had Paul read in the Bible that God set him apart for the particular work he was sending him out to accomplish? Do you know of a verse that told Paul he should go forth? Remember, at that time they only had the Old Testament. The New Testament hadn't been written yet. Do you see instead that the *Holy Spirit* spoke directly to Paul and Barnabas? They didn't read about this in the Bible."

After pondering the question a moment, Ken remarked, "You know Bill, you have a point. This was a direct word from the Holy Spirit. I'll have to give some more thought to this concept."

Paul's personal word from God in Acts 13 had come as they worshipped, and it spoke specifically to Paul and Barnabas. Speaking into our lives is part of the Holy Spirit's work. Let's consider this further.

The Holy Spirit's Work In Us

Have you ever wondered what the Holy Spirit's work is within a believer? The Bible tells us that when we first believe, God seals us with the Holy Spirit as a sign of ownership and a guarantee of eternal life (Eph. 1:13). Further, we are told in Ephesians 5:18 to be filled with the Spirit. What a wonderful gift. We can be filled with the very presence of God Himself through the Holy Spirit. This One, whose character radiates love and compassion, actually lives within every believer. That means that God's amazing love is available to us any time we call on Him.

God is thoroughly invested in and devoted to each of His children. He cares about every aspect of our lives and offers us an intimate personal relationship. The Holy Spirit is there to cheer us on in our faith walk, to encourage us toward right choices, and to inspire us to love one another. He turns our hearts to Jesus, to know Him more, to seek His heart.

I was reflecting on Psalm 27:4, *"One thing I have asked from the Lord, that I shall seek: That I may dwell in the house of the Lord all the days of my life, to behold the <u>beauty</u> of the Lord and to meditate in His temple."*

The word 'beauty' stood out to me (a rhema word). I began to wonder exactly what was meant by *the beauty of the Lord*. I didn't think it was referring to outward beauty because that sounded kind of shallow, and Isaiah 53:2 indicates that *"...He (Jesus) has no stately form or majesty that we should look upon Him, nor appearance that we should be attracted to Him."*

Granted that may have been true when Jesus was in His earthly body, especially during the ravages of the crucifixion, but when we see Him, He will be full of splendor and majesty. His beauty will be outward and inward. Jesus Himself said in John 17:24 *"Father, I desire that they also, whom You have given Me, be with Me where I am, so that they may see My glory which You have given Me, for You loved Me before the foundation of the world."* Jesus longs for us to see the beauty of His glory in eternity, but I felt in the Psalms passage, there might be further meaning to the word beauty.

So, I looked it up in Hebrew on my computer Bible program and was very surprised by the definition. The root word for beauty in Hebrew means: to be agreeable, to be a delight, pleasant, and sweet.

There it is. The biblical meaning of Jesus' beauty is that He is an agreeable person who is pleasant to be around, and is sweet. I then contemplated what it meant for Jesus to be agreeable. Bill helped me put an interesting slant on it by pointing out that when something is agreeable, that means it fits. Jesus work on the cross is a perfect fit to our need for a Savior. Jesus is agreeable in being the answer to all of our needs, and in doing so, he is both pleasant and sweet. That thought sounds so attractive, so appealing, so becoming and inviting.

Who wouldn't want to be around a person with such likeable qualities? I love being around people who are agreeable, pleasant, and sweet. Don't you? There is such warmth in that thought, that Jesus, living in us by the Holy Spirit, is relentlessly kind and tenderhearted in his sweet nature, continuously filled with gentleness and compassion. I am captivated by this revelation.

In that moment, the Holy Spirit spoke to me that He, too, is exactly like that. Agreeable, pleasant, and sweet.

Then, what is the purpose of this lovely, genial person, the Holy Spirit? What has God promised from our relationship with the third person of the Trinity? John 14:16-17 tells us. *"I will ask the Father,*

*and He will give you another Helper, that He may be with you forever;
that is the Spirit of truth...."*

One of the Holy Spirit's works in us is to help us know the truth.
Like me, perhaps you have found that it is easier to hear truth if it is
given by a person who is kindhearted, gentle, and tender, one who
handles your emotions with care. That is the work of the Holy Spirit
in us.

If He assists us in truth, we might ask how He does this. Jesus
said, *"I have many more things to say to you...when He, the Spirit
of truth, comes, He will guide you into all the truth; for He will not
speak on His own initiative, but whatever He hears, He will speak;
and He will disclose to you what is to come. He shall glorify Me; for
He shall take of Mine, and shall disclose it to you..."* (Jn. 16:12-15).

These verses explain that there are many things this sweet Holy
Spirit needs to teach us and guide us toward. Notice it says guide, not
push. He wants to engage us in our daily walk. We can be confident
in trusting Him because His character and love for us are impeccable.

But how does He disclose truth to us? Jesus promised the Holy
Spirit would disclose things to us that we do not presently know. As
we seek God about the issues of our lives, the Holy Spirit takes the
answers from God and speaks them to our heart. Therefore, we need
to be listening so we don't miss what God has to say. This vital, but
often neglected, role is unique to the Holy Spirit. The Lord wants to
speak to us, but we must be tuned in to receive what He has to tell us.

What Keeps Us From Hearing?

In a recent newspaper article, I read about two boys who nearly
drowned in a local lake. Ice broke beneath their feet plunging them
into the freezing water. Nearby, several fishermen were spending
a cozy afternoon in their fishing huts on the lake. They heard the
sounds of the boys yelling for help but mistook the noise for the cry
of geese flying overhead.

One fisherman, upon emerging from his hut to view the geese, saw that it wasn't geese at all, but drowning children causing the commotion. Hurriedly, he found help and saved the boys.

Everyday, we hear many voices. The voices of radio, television, magazines, newspapers, and other people all vie for our attention. With so many voices bombarding our lives each day, how can we discern the voice of God? How often have we mistaken His voice for the call of geese?

Suppose we turn on a radio with the intent of listening to some Christian music. We find that many other stations compete for our attention - rock music stations, western music, classical music, talk shows and news are just a few. Because we are familiar with the sound of Christian music, we quickly pass by other stations until we recognize the appropriate songs.

The purpose of this book is to help us recognize God's voice in our daily lives, to instill the thought that it is perfectly normal to hear God's voice. Our personal relationship with God, after all, is dependent in large part upon our ability to listen to Him.

God not only wants to speak to us, but probably does so more often than we might imagine. May this book help to fine tune our listening abilities so that we will put the geese aside and hear what God has to say. Blessings are sure to follow. *"Blessed is the man who listens to me, watching daily at my gates, waiting at my doorposts"* (Prov. 8:34).

It was once asked, "Is it that God doesn't speak, or is it that we don't hear?" This concept became clear one afternoon when I took my son, Mike, and his friend to the ice skating rink. The rink's location was on the lower level of a two story mall. The upper level served as a balcony overlooking the rink.

Leaving the boys to skate, I spent the afternoon shopping. Several times during the day, I returned to the rink to see how they were doing. On one occasion, I looked down from the upper level and saw they were having a wonderful time gliding along the ice. Other friends from their school had joined them making it a fun afternoon. As I peered over the balcony, at one point, I cupped my hands over my mouth and called out, "Mike." But due to the loud music below and Mike's unawareness of my presence, he kept skating. Again, I shouted out his name trying to get his attention. Everyone on the upper level heard me, but Mike went on absorbed in his skating. Not expecting me to call out to him, he wasn't watching for or expecting to hear my voice.

Although I delighted in watching Mike enjoy a carefree afternoon, I felt frustrated at my inability to contact him from my position above. I began to think that, in a crude way, this may sometimes define our relationship with God. He looks down from heaven and sees us enjoying life. We aren't necessarily doing anything wrong, but we may not be tuned to hear His voice. Similar to my experience with Mike, God wants us to look up.

Repeatedly in the book of Matthew, Jesus says, *"He who has ears, let him hear"* (Mt.13:9). Could it be that we, like the disciples, have ears but at times fail to tune in to hear God's voice? God's desire is that we expect to hear His voice in our daily lives. He wants us to be on the alert, watching and listening for a word from Him. Our Christian walk has the potential to be one of excitement, adventure, and blessing when we begin to anticipate that, indeed, God does want to speak to us.

Twice in Proverbs 8, the phrase, "I call" is used in reference to God initiating a call in the voice of wisdom. *"Does not wisdom call, and understanding lift up her voice"* (Prov. 8:1)? Again in verse 4 *"To you, O men, I call, and my voice is to the sons of men."*

Cookbook for Kim

A good example of one who listened well involves our daughter, Kim, and a lady in her church. You will see in this story how God used a 'listening' woman to bless Kim. God's provision sometimes comes to us through another person as He speaks to them in a still, small voice. Not every word from God is for a life changing event. Sometimes, God looks for opportunities to bless His children in little ways. Recently married, Kim wanted to do a good job of cooking for her husband, John. She prayed that the Lord would provide a cookbook, but the one she found cost ten dollars. Since John was finishing college and they lived within a tight budget, she felt that price was more than she could afford at that time. So, she continued praying.

That Sunday, she discovered her church was selling cookbooks, and they cost only six dollars. John agreed she could get one after the service. As she took her seat in church, Kim noticed the lady next to her had purchased one of the cookbooks, so she asked if she could look through it. What an unexpected blessing when, after the service, the woman leaned over to Kim and said, "I've sensed the Lord telling me to give you this cookbook. Please, consider it yours." Kim was delighted not only to have her prayer answered but to know that this woman had heard from God and obeyed.

Such a simple incident, yet sometimes the Lord chooses to use us to provide for the needs of others. If we make the decision to watch for opportunities, we will soon find God opening doors of blessing that we never would have imagined.

God Speaks Today

God still speaks personally to His people today. We are His sheep and we can still hear His voice. If He spoke to Adam, Moses, David, Paul and many others in the Bible, He can speak to us too. How full and rich life becomes when we begin to tap in on all the wonderful things God wants to tell us. I love when I'm teaching and He drops a new thought into my mind, or when I'm mentoring someone and a fresh solution seems to pop up. When it lines up with biblical principles, a word can be wholeheartedly embraced.

When a friend, pastor, or teacher says something that sheds light on a troublesome issue, who are we really hearing from? I believe we have all heard God's voice many times. He cares so much about each of us. Because a word often comes in such ordinary ways, we might not recognize that God has spoken. His voice frequently fits in with everyday life. Let's take a step of faith, expecting God to speak to us.

Study Guide 1

1. What are some ways God can speak to us?

2. How do the following verses connect with hearing from God?
   A. Psalm 27:14
   B. Ecclesiastes 5:1-2

3. Is it Biblical to hear God's voice?
   A. Hebrews 1:1-2
   B. John 10:27
   C. John 8:47

4. A. What do these verses tell about rhema words? (These are four of the 70 plus times rhema is used in the New Testament.)
   Rom.10:17
   Eph. 5:26, 6:17
   Matt. 4:4
   B. How does a rhema word differ from the logos word?

5. A. Explain Paul's experience in Acts 13:2-3.
   B. How did God speak to Paul?

6. How does the Holy Spirit disclose truth to us?

7. Tell the command given in Mark 4:9.

8. What could hinder a person from hearing God's voice?

9. How is Malachi 3:6 an assurance that God speaks today?

CHAPTER 2

Faith Comes From Hearing

"So faith comes from hearing, and hearing by the word of Christ" (Rom.10:17).

Moving to Southern California

IN CHAPTER ONE, we looked at verses and testimonies that point out God's intention for us to hear His voice. Let's go a step further and ask this question: What is the outcome of hearing God's voice? What is one of God's main purposes when He is speaking to us? In this next account, observe what God was building in me.

We had lived in our Walnut Creek, CA home, the one that endured the fire and mud, for about a year and a half. Now, a move to Southern California was on the horizon. We had prayed and counseled with friends and felt it was God's will for us to move. While excited in some ways, emotionally it was a hard decision. Transferring to a new location, we soon faced the task of finding a place to live.

On our first exploratory trip south, the weather was overcast and rainy. The September day looked dull and gray, affecting our mood as we drove to our first stop in the northern part of Los Angeles County.

So this was 'sunny,' Southern California. Certainly, this gloomy, drizzly day wasn't ideal for house hunting.

With so many communities in Southern California, literally hundreds in Los Angeles County alone, our first challenge was an attempt to select a town. As we drove along, I began to reminisce about our time in Northern California. We had met the Lord shortly after moving there, raised our girls, and made wonderful friends in our church.

We had lived there eleven years, enough time to develop a rapport with many people, sharing our joys and struggles. How accustomed and dependent we had become on their support. They were like family to us. These had been good years. I groaned as I realized that I'd no longer be able to talk for hours with Nancy or Carol. No more spur of the moment dinners with Kathy and Tom. Everything and everyone would be new. I was convinced we would feel lonely for awhile. The children would have adjustments to make with new friends and schools. Would they fit in and be happy? Would Bill find contentment and fulfillment in his new job? Would there be any Christians in our new community? Would we find a church and areas of ministry? Bill had even joked with friends, "I don't think God could use me in Southern California." So many unanswered questions loomed before us.

In our town of Walnut Creek, we knew just where to shop to find what we needed. We knew all the short cuts and back streets. Lots of adjustments and changes lay ahead. Questions swirled in my mind, like the clouds that hung low in the sky that day. Adventure and excitement quickly waned as nostalgic feelings washed over me. As we traveled from town to town, neighborhood to neighborhood, we soon became confused. How could we choose a town, much less a neighborhood, when the selection was so large and nothing really looked like home?

The first area the realtor showed us was Newhall, north of L.A. They had recently experienced a large earthquake and some of the freeways had collapsed. We immediately crossed that town off our list and moved on to several other options.

After a fruitless day of house hunting, we felt discouraged. Returning to the home of friends we were staying with, we felt the strain and pressure of the day's events. Teary eyed, I dismissed myself to an early bed time. I needed some "one on one time" with the Lord. I needed to hear His voice.

Curling up on the bed, I began my lament. *Oh Lord, You see how distressed and downcast I've become about this move. We thought it was Your will but never expected it to be like this. There is no place to live, and I don't even like it here. I miss my friends already. Lord, do you really want us to move? Have we misread Your will? Please, give me a word of comfort and encouragement.*

Lazily, I reached over to the bedside table and picked up my Bible. Turning the pages, not knowing where to read, I leafed through the Psalms. As the pages turned, chapter 107 caught my eye, so I paused to read it. Within a few verses, my mouth dropped open in amazement. The message was so personal, so timely. I quickly recognized that God was speaking directly to me from this ancient text.

Beginning with verse 3, *"And* (He) *gathered* (them) *from the lands, from the east and from the west, from the north, and from the south."*

Yes, I thought. *He had gathered us from Northern California alright.*

Verse 4, *"They wandered in the wilderness in a desert region."*

Hmmm, I pondered...*We had wandered all day in a desert region.*

Southern California is considered high desert. Lots of open space surrounds the population. Common sights are dry, scruffy terrain, cactus, sand, and rock. Maybe not just like a desert but Bill says, "more like the "Badlands." If you recall the old western movies, they were often filmed in Southern California.

I read on. *"They did not find a way to an inhabited city."*

By now, God had my full attention. Indeed, again, that was us! We had roamed all over Los Angeles County and couldn't even find a city that seemed right to us.

Verse 5, *"They were hungry and thirsty; their soul fainted within them."*

My sentiments exactly! I began to sense that God knew exactly what we were going through. His eye was upon us. I eagerly read on.

Verse 6, *"Then they cried out to the Lord in their trouble; He delivered them out of their distress."*

Encouragement at last! A promise from the Lord. I'd take it.

Verse 7, *"He led them also by a straight way, to go to an inhabited city."*

What a personal word. A promise that the Lord was going to provide. He was going to lead us to a city. Overwhelmed by God's personal concern and love, I asked Him what He wanted from me. Verses 8 and 22 gave me the answer.

"Let them give thanks to the Lord for His lovingkindness, and for His wonders to the sons of men (vs. 8). Let them also offer sacrifices of thanksgiving, and tell of His works with joyful singing" (vs. 22).

Brought short by my negative, "woe is me" attitude, I realized there had been no thankfulness in my heart the whole day. I asked God's forgiveness and began to offer a sacrifice of thanksgiving.

Remember, nothing had changed in our outward circumstances. It was still a dreary day, and we still had nowhere to move. Yet, God had just given me a rhema word directly from the Bible, a word tailor-made for our specific situation.

Thankfulness is easy when all is going well, but God wanted thanks when, from my perspective, our world was falling apart. Granted, it's hard to give thanks in the midst of turmoil and struggle. Our heart might not be in it and our mind might say it's unreasonable. In these times, by an act of our will, we can offer a sacrifice of thanksgiving.

Ephesians 5:20 exhorts us to have the mindset of *"always giving thanks for all things in the name of our Lord Jesus Christ to God, even the Father."* This is an act of gratitude, offered by faith, regardless of feelings. It's a choice that says, *I believe You are in the midst of this trial and that You have it all figured out. Therefore, I choose to trust You and thank You.*

Hebrews 11, the "Hall of Faith" chapter, begins with a definition of faith and points to godly men who walked in biblical faith. The first verse defines faith as *"...the assurance of things hoped for, the conviction of things not seen."*

Even though we had not seen it, I began to thank the Lord in the midst of our unsettled situation, sad feelings and exhaustion. I thanked Him that He was still in control and still had a plan. Upon offering this sacrifice of thanks, my heart began to settle. My soul quieted and my distress abated.

As I read on, I claimed verse 30 as a promise. *"...So He guided them to their desired haven."* A promise which was now personal. I trusted that in His time He would bring it about.

We returned home for several months. At the end of December, we returned to Southern California, as a family, for more house hunting. We felt hopeful. The sun was shining and it was a beautiful, warm day.

Our cheery realtor led us to the first house of the day in the city of Thousand Oaks. My anticipation grew as I recalled God's promise from Psalm 107. I felt at peace, assured that God was present with us and would lead us just as He promised. I also recalled Psalm 31:3, *"For You are my rock and my fortress; For Your name's sake You will lead me and guide me."* It pays to trust the Lord. He never fails in His plans for us.

We immediately liked the town and the neighborhood our realtor showed us. After inspecting the house, a two story, newly built home with lots of land, we all agreed this would be a good option. Excitement grew as we envisioned our furniture in place inside and landscaping and a pool, outside. In one day, God had provided a city, and a house. Not only a place to dwell but a *desired haven*, one we loved, just as He promised in Psalm 107:30. Again, we gave thanks, only this time it wasn't a sacrifice. We excitedly looked forward to our move and the new, stretching experiences God would bring into each of our lives.

Reflection

Let's take a moment to review this situation of hearing from God through Scripture. I felt a need to hear God's voice for direction, comfort, and reassurance, to know that God was with us in our pursuit of a house. These were all practical needs. When I began seeking God in the Scriptures, I expected to hear from Him. I had excused myself from a social evening with the distinct purpose of seeking God's help.

Jeremiah 29:12-13 says, *"Then you will call upon Me and come and pray to Me, and I will listen to you. And you will seek Me and find Me, when you search for Me with all your heart."* When I sought Jesus with focused attention, I found Him in the midst of my struggle. He gave me encouragement, hope, and a sense of relief. Then, He directed me to thank Him as He built my faith.

As we think about the matter of faith and the way the Lord chooses to build it, let's pause to consider where faith comes from. Being led to a Scripture that directly applied to my situation, it built my faith and trust that God was with me. It became a rhema word just for me. In truth, every time God speaks into my life, my faith is built. Let's look further into this idea.

Where Does Faith Come From?

Romans 10:17 states, *"So faith comes from hearing, and hearing by the word of Christ."* In Greek, *word* in this verse is again rhema. This verse is saying that faith is built by hearing rhema from God. Pause a moment and consider the significance of that truth. Our faith is broadened and increases as we hear personal words from the Lord. Hearing from God has the potential to grow and expand our faith.

Faith was initially implanted and began to grow in each of us when we first heard the good news of the gospel and received Christ as our personal Lord and Savior. But there is more. We must nurture that faith, cultivate it, and allow it to mature by spending time with the Lord, seeking to know Him, and feeding on His Word. As we begin to recognize God's voice, faith is strengthened and enlarged. If we think about the times in our lives when our faith has been built the most, it's usually those times when we sensed that God had somehow intervened personally with a distinct word for a specific situation.

Conversely, if faith wanes, while it could be due to lack of prayer and fellowship, time in the Bible, or sin, perhaps another reason could be failure to hear God's voice. If hearing God's voice builds faith, then could a deficit of hearing reduce faith? Some Christians walk through life defeated, without hope, discouraged, and possibly unaware that their relationship with God is hampered because they have not recognized His voice.

Sadly, what can happen in this situation is that relationship with God is replaced with rigid rules, laws and religious rituals. When God's voice is not heard, legalism tends to take over and can become a stronghold. An attitude of "do's and don'ts" replaces relationship and leads to spiritual bondage. God is not stiff and unapproachable. He is all about relationship, and relationship, by its very nature, pre-supposes communication.

In Amos 8:11 we are told of Israel's experience in captivity. *"Behold, days are coming," declares the Lord God, "when I will send a famine on the land, not a famine for bread or a thirst for water, but rather for hearing the words of the Lord."* This prophecy was fulfilled before Jesus' birth and lasted four hundred years. Not a word from God was heard during that era. Thankfully, we are not living in a time of famine for hearing God's words. However, there are some who live in self-imposed deprivation, in a state of spiritual starvation.

Just as Amos received a word about spiritual famine, many people in the Bible received other personal words from the Lord. Dialogue with God was a common, if not a normal life experience. Encouraged and built up in faith, God's children thrived as they heeded the Father's voice. So, before I continue with stories from my life, let's look at the accounts of some biblical people.

Did Anyone In the Bible Hear God's Voice?

It is important for us to look at the Scriptures to discern if hearing God's voice was a normal experience for people in Bible times. If it was normal for them, then it should be normal for us because God is the same today as He was yesterday. I can think of no place in Scripture where we are told that God no longer speaks to His children. Let's listen to some of their testimonies.

Noah spent a hundred years of his life working on a major project. Why did Noah build the ark? What caused him to have a compelling conviction to devote such a large chunk of time on this task? Why would he be willing to undergo hardship and the torment of abusive people for decades when there had never been a drop of rain and the word 'flood' was likely not in their vocabulary?

The answer is that Noah had received a rhema word, a personal word from God. *"Then God said to Noah, 'The end of all flesh has come before Me; for the earth is filled with violence because of them; and behold I am about to destroy them with the earth. Make for yourself an ark of gopher wood...'"* (Gen. 6:13-14).

Through that word, God built Noah's faith. A faith that was so strong that despite hardship, mocking, and persecution, Noah determined to fulfill what God had revealed to him. With the word came the power to be obedient.

Interestingly, Noah's name means *rest* or *comfort*. He rested in the Lord's word, trusting God for deliverance. God used Noah to deliver his family from judgment and destruction and to give mankind a second chance.

Abraham also received a rhema word. Certain that he had heard a personal word from God, he left his homeland and wandered as an alien in a foreign land for many years. *"Now the Lord said to Abram, 'go forth from your country, and from your relatives and from your father's house, to the land which I will show you'"* (Gen. 12:1). Abraham didn't dream up this plan to move on his own initiative. God spoke to him and he obeyed.

He received another word from the Lord regarding a child. That word came to pass when Isaac was born. Romans 4:20-21 gives understanding of how important God's word was to Abraham when it says of him, *"Yet, with respect to the promise of God, he did not waver in unbelief, but grew strong in faith, giving glory to God, and being fully assured that what He had promised, He was able also to perform."*

Abraham's faith increased when he received his rhema word. However, it should be noted that, although he did not waver in faith, he did not obey God's word but took things into his own hands. Knowing he was getting old and wanting this promised son, he went ahead of God's timing. With Sarah's blessing, he had Ishmael with Sarah's maid, Hagar. Still, when God gives a word, He has a plan and nothing will ultimately thwart that plan. Abraham's promised son, Isaac, was born thirteen years later. *"For the Lord Almighty has purposed, and who can thwart him? His hand is stretched out, and who can turn it back"* (Isa 14:27). (NIV)

Joseph heard God's voice in a dream. Though he met with many difficult situations in his life, he chose to believe God's rhema word to him. If anyone ever had reason to waver in their faith, Joseph did. He was rejected by his brothers, thrown into a pit, sold to the Ishmaelites, unjustly accused and thrown in a dungeon. His circumstances had the potential to trigger immense stress and doubt, yet he remained steadfast in faith. Why?

Despite Joseph's hardships, God used these events in his life to shape his character and attitude. Joseph never forgot what God had spoken to him. He looked at his trials as the working out of God's plan for his life. He coped without complaint or bitterness because he had heard the voice of God early in his life, and he chose to allow God to accomplish His will. (To read about God's promise to Joseph, begin in Genesis 37).

In Exodus 3, Moses had a conversation with God. God spoke personally to him concerning direction for his life and His plans for Israel. Though Moses resisted God's plan at first, he eventually chose to step out in faith and lead the Israelites out of Egypt. God reaffirmed His promises to him, and by faith Moses executed many mighty exploits. As he acted on the words God had spoken to him, Moses' faith grew.

Yet, another example was when God called Samuel by name and had a personal conversation with him concerning coming events in Israel. Samuel's faith matured from this revelation. *"Thus Samuel grew and the Lord was with him and let none of his words fail"* (I Sam. 3:19). Cultivating a deep relationship with the Lord through their frequent conversations, Samuel became one of the foremost judges in the land of Israel. Interestingly, *"...a word from the Lord was rare in those days, visions were infrequent"* (I Sam. 3:1). But God had an eager listener in Samuel.

Joshua heard the voice of the Lord when God told him to cross the Jordan and enter the Promised Land. *"Have I not commanded you? Be strong and courageous! Do not tremble or be dismayed, for the Lord your God is with you wherever you go"* (Josh. 1:9). Tenderly, the Lord reassured Joshua that He would be with him and would not forsake him. These words, along with the renewed promise, gave Joshua the faith he needed to go in and possess the land.

Moving to the New Testament, Mary received a rhema word from God that she would be the mother of Jesus, the awaited Messiah. Mary's word from God came through an angel. *"And the angel said to her, 'Do not be afraid, Mary; for you have found favor with God. And behold, you will conceive in your womb, and bear a son, and you shall name Him Jesus'"* (Lk. 1:30-31). Mary pondered God's word in her heart, and she treasured it.

Near that time, Zacharias also received a word from the Lord by way of an angel. He was told that his wife Elizabeth would have a son, and he should be called John. *"But the angel said to him, 'Do not be afraid, Zacharias, for your petition has been heard, and your wife Elizabeth will bear you a son, and you will give him the name John'"* (Lk. 1:13). Zacharias was struck mute until his son arrived because, at first, he doubted God's word. But again, God followed through with His promise. The faith of both of these families increased as they anticipated the arrival of their prophesied babies.

In Luke 5:4-6 we recount the story of the disciples on a fishing trip. Though they had fished all night, they had caught nothing. Jesus then told Simon, *"Put out into the deep and let down your nets for a catch."* Simon answered, *"Master, we toiled all night and took nothing! But at your <u>word</u> I will let down the nets"* (RSV). As they followed Jesus' word, their faith soared. Great quantities of fish were snatched from the sea, even to the point of breaking their nets. Again, the Lord's word was accomplished and became a building block to their faith.

Several points make this story interesting. First, Peter accomplished nothing in his fishing attempts before he heard from Jesus. Second, *word* is again rhema in the Greek. *"...But at your <u>word</u> I will let down the nets"* (Lk. 5:5). Peter received a personal word directly from the Lord that applied to his specific situation. Third, when Peter applied the word he found success.

When we hear a distinct word from the Lord, that word contains the power to accomplish what is said. In Jeremiah1:12, God promises, *"...I am watching over My word to perform it."* God is always true to His word. Whatever proceeds from His mouth will be done. Like Jeremiah, Peter learned that to receive and act on the words of Jesus assured success. God always honors His word.

When God gives a word, we can know that He has gone ahead of the word and prepared the way. With Peter, God had already prepared a load of fish ready to enter the net. From Peter's viewpoint, it seemed impossible that any fish could be nearby. After all, he had already fished all night. He had done his best.

Peter's success encourages us as well. When things seem impossible from our viewpoint, yet we hear from God, we can be sure He will act. The integrity and character of God is trustworthy. Faith is built as we hear God's word and believe it.

Another biblical example of God's rhema occurred at the Pool of Bethesda. John 5:2-9 says, *"Now there is in Jerusalem by the sheep gate a pool, which is called in Hebrew Bethesda, having five porticoes. In these lay a multitude of those who were sick, blind, lame, and withered, waiting for the moving of the waters; for an angel of the Lord went down at certain seasons into the pool and stirred up the water; whoever then first, after the stirring up of the water, stepped in was made well from whatever disease with which he was afflicted. A man was there who had been ill for thirty-eight years. When Jesus saw him lying there, and knew that he had already been a long time in that condition, He said to him, 'Do you wish to get well?' The sick man answered Him, 'Sir, I have no man to put me into the pool when the water is stirred up, but while I am coming, another steps down before me.' Jesus said to him, 'Get up, pick up your pallet and walk.' Immediately the man became well, and picked up his pallet and began to walk."*

This is a classic story of Jesus seeing a need, offering a simple, practical, personal word and following up with a powerful healing. Upon learning that the crippled man desired to be healed, Jesus rhema was to "g*et up, pick up your pallet and walk.*" It was a short, concise, and easily understood word. Nothing complicated about it. The man obeyed. He chose to get up and walk, and he was healed. Case closed.

Countless other biblical characters also heard God's voice. For many of them, it was a natural part of their lives and they responded quickly. Other times, as in the case of Jonah, the response was not so fast. Hearing from God and responding promptly is a skill to be cultivated.

There is an interesting principle at work in the lives of biblical characters who heard God's voice. There appears to be a thread that ties many of their experiences together, a similar theme emerging from their situations. More often than not, it seems more likely that God spoke to people whose hearts were attuned to Him. These were not the "name it and claim it" folks who considered God their ticket to abundant material possessions but people who walked with authentic faith, people who would agree to participate in accomplishing His will. While any believer can hear God's voice, we need to ask an important question: Why would God entrust a word to someone who was not seeking Him, someone who lived life on the edge of Christianity, perhaps double minded or disingenuous? II Timothy

2:2 puts it well *"The things which you have heard from me in the presence of many witnesses, entrust these to faithful men who will be able to teach others also."*

Rethink each of the biblical characters we just read about who heard from God. What kind of people were they? Granted, they were not perfect, but they had something in common. Most displayed genuine, heartfelt faith and a willingness to risk following God. Noah endured the torment of his fellow citizens. To them he looked like an idiot. Yet he was strong in faith. Abraham counted following God as more important than living near family. Joseph was willing to suffer the torture of a dungeon and unfair accusations to serve God. Moses allowed God to use him to save his people. Mary took the chance of being ostracized when found pregnant outside of wedlock. Peter could have looked like a fool in the fishing incident, but chose to be obedient. The lame man at the pool took the risk of trusting God by following His command to get up and walk.

Each of these people, when they received a word from God, had to count the cost. Then, they had to step out in faith and obey. In each case, they experienced God's faithfulness to His word.

We have the same decision. Are we willing to walk in sincerity of faith? If called to, are we willing to take a risk for God? If God does speak to us, are we prepared to obey? God is looking for a heart that is fully His. *"For the eyes of the Lord move to and fro throughout the earth that He may strongly support those whose heart is completely His"* (IIChron. 16:9).

Usually, a word from God has an 'if-then' clause requiring a step of faith before the word comes about. Some people who have sensed a call and have spent time considering and pondering the feasibility of the idea, then abandon it. Possibly, other people reinforced their word with excitement. But as time went on and they counted the cost, measuring the changes required, they ultimately decided not to take the risk. Changes such as moving, purchasing land, or having someone live with them can sound daunting. While they may never know what blessings could have been experienced, God can still continue to prosper their local ministry. Sometimes, we're left with the question of whether God had really spoken to them. In some cases, it would seem so. When they didn't act, was God mad at them? I doubt it. But they may have missed a blessing.

It should be noted that when we sense God leading us in a direction, it is prudent to seek wise counsel from godly Christians before moving forward. Especially when a word involves a lifestyle change. There is safety in many counselors. *"Without consultation, plans are frustrated, But with many counselors they succeed"* (Prov. 15:22).

Many words we receive don't give the details of timing or implementation. We don't always see clearly how to proceed. In some cases it would be irresponsible to move forward without a plan of action, without first counting the cost and thinking through the process. *"How blessed is the man who finds wisdom and the man who gains understanding"* (Prov. 3:13). While some words are fairly simple and easily followed such as "call Carol, or write a note of encouragement to Jim," words like "sell everything and move to Ethiopia" might need further confirmation.

Mike and Favor

When we were raising Mike, it was important to us to build character, conscience and faith into him. We knew these principles, along with others, would carry him well in life, and indeed they have. Bill's approach was to teach Mike through practical biblical principles, often with true stories and word pictures which brought them to life.

One of the habits I formed early with him took place in the mornings as he ate his breakfast before heading off to school. We would sit together for about twenty minutes, and I would either read the Bible to him, help him work on memory verses, pray with him, sing worship songs together, or sometimes read faith building Guidepost stories. We had a variety of venues that we alternated so as to keep our quiet time fresh each morning. There was one thing that I consistently did before he left for school, however. Each day,

I ended our prayer time with this prayer, *Lord, please be with Mike today and give him favor with his teacher and with the other students.*

Mike is an adult now with his own family, but as I look back over the years, I can see how God used that simple prayer to speak to his heart and direct decisions he made. Not only did God answer my prayer regarding favor for Mike, but He also used it to strategically place some important building blocks in his life.

When Mike was in later grade school, because he was a respected, responsible student, he was asked not only to be a crossing guard, but also tasked with the duty of lieutenant. Only three students were honored with this position. Mike took seriously the authority he had been given. At one point, there was a defiant student who reported to his mother that Mike had threatened him at the school crossing. The next morning, Mike was called to the principal's office where the mother accused Mike of threatening her son. The principal asked Mike if that was what happened, to which Mike replied, "No, that is not true."

After listening to both sides, the principal made his decision, "I know both of these boys," he said. "I have watched them at school and I believe Mike."

Because the principal knew Mike to be a person of integrity and the other boy was known as a trouble maker, the principal believed Mike. God gave Mike favor. Character counts.

That was the beginning of Mike choosing a "Life Verse," from the Bible, one that has carried him well in many circumstances. Proverbs 22:1, *"A good name is to be more desired than great wealth, Favor is better than silver and gold."*

Over the years, our church offered mission trips to the Dominican Republic, and Mike was able to participate in several of these trips. As part of each student's ministry there, they were asked to prepare a short teaching. As you may guess, Mike spoke on favor, especially the favor extended to young people as they choose to obey their parents. He told how following that standard had frequently brought blessings into his life.

When Mike went to college, I began to have doubts that I had done enough to prepare him for adulthood. I hoped he would make right decisions now that he was away from home, but I was concerned that our training might have fallen short. I didn't tell anyone about my anxious thoughts but prayed that the Lord would help Mike to make good choices.

One day, a friend knocked on my door. When I answered, she seemed to want to talk to me about something but admitted she felt a little awkward and unsettled as to whether what she wanted to say would make any sense. "Betsy, as I've been praying, I've felt the Lord has given me a word for you." By then, I was all ears. What could God want to tell me that caused my friend to drive across town yet feel uncomfortable in expressing herself?

Finally, quick and to the point, she shared what the Lord had imparted to her. "From what I'm hearing from the Lord," she began, "I'm wondering if you might need to know that everything you have built into Mike in his early years, he is now walking in."

I could tell she was wondering if that was even an issue I was concerned about. She went on to explain that God wanted me to know that nothing was lost, that Mike was a strong person today and what we had taught him over the years was enough.

I was amazed at her words. I had not told a soul of my inner conflict, yet God had heard my prayer and brought a friend to the door to comfort and affirm me. Her words put my heart at ease. I no longer felt the turmoil that had been nagging at me regarding this issue. God cared enough to bring words of consolation through a caring friend, words that brought a refreshing peace to my soul.

After college, Mike went to work for a financial services company. Because he had performed well in sales in his region, he was given the honor of bringing a speech to a gathering of company employees and executives. I asked Mike what he planned to speak on. Without hesitation, he answered, "I'm going to speak on favor using my life verse, Proverbs 22:1, *A good name is to be more desired than great wealth, Favor is better than silver and gold.*" He would be explaining that his philosophy was that it is more important to be a person of character than to make lots of money. He knew that if his clients trusted him, he would find favor with them.

That verse from Proverbs has been strategic in moving Mike into his destiny. Today, Mike has his own investment counseling business and continues to reap from what God sowed in his heart many years ago from a simple prayer of a mother's heart. *Lord, give him favor with his teachers and the other students.*

Of course, my prayer has adjusted over the years to better match his present circumstances. Mike continues to find favor and believes Proverbs 22:1 was truly given to him by God and has directed many decisions in his life.

Having seen that faith comes from hearing and having seen that not only did God speak to people in biblical days but also to us today, let's move on to some stories of how God specifically speaks through His Word today.

Study Guide 2

1. What are some personal things you would like to hear from God?

2. Share an assuring promise from Jeremiah 29:12-13.

3. A. Where does faith come from? Romans 10:17
   B. How is "word" unique in this verse?
   C. If faith wanes, what could be the reason?

4. What kind of self-imposed famine do we sometimes live in? Amos 8:11

5. A. Name several people from the Old Testament who received a personal word from God.
   1) Genesis 6:13
   2) Genesis 12:1-4
   3) I Samuel 3
   4) Judges 13
   B. Chart your observations as to how hearing from God affected them personally.

6. Name several people from the New Testament who heard God's voice, and tell how it changed their lives.

7. A. Think about the meaning of this statement: "When we hear a distinct word from the Lord, that word contains the power to accomplish what is said."
   B. Apply this statement to Peter in these verses.
   1) Luke 5:4-6
   2) Matthew 14:22-29
   C. Apply this statement to a situation in your life.

CHAPTER 3

God Speaks Through Scripture

*"...I am watching over My word
to perform it" (Jer. 1:12).*

Hearing God through the Bible

I HAVE TO ADMIT, my favorite way to hear God's voice is through a Bible verse or section of Scripture. You can probably understand why, after He spoke so clearly to me in our house hunting experience in Southern California. God aptly personalized Psalm 107 on that occasion. My expectation had been high, and my attention focused.

Sometimes, we're not expecting to hear from God, but with a little reflection, we realize that a reference to a Bible verse was the first step to a changed attitude, a response or direction in our life. A quote I once heard seems appropriate: *"If you want to hear from God, read your Bible; if you want to audibly hear from God, read your Bible out loud."* The following story depicts a decision made on the basis of a biblical principle that set in motion a life changing course for our daughter, Kim's, future.

Dating Dilemma

Being a tall, attractive blond, our oldest daughter, Kim, rarely lacked for dates in high school. The young men she dated were quality friends for her in every way but one. Many did not share her Christian faith. I'll let Kim tell her story from her point of view.

Kim: When I began dating in high school, at first my parents felt it seemed harmless for me to go out with non-Christian boys as friends. Mostly, dating involved group events. At one point, I met a great guy I'll call Paul, who was nice looking, athletic, and had many positive character qualities. My parents liked him. Our relationship started as a fun friendship, but as time went by, it began to grow into something more. We really cared for each other. We saw each other at school, and in the evenings, we often had long phone conversations.

As we talked late into the night, our conversations focused more and more on me trying to convince him of the value of a relationship with Jesus. Sadly, our discussions became increasingly frustrating as he continued to resist the plan of salvation. I knew my parents were concerned.

"Mom, I am talking to Paul about the Lord," I explained. "I realize that even though he attends a church in town, he doesn't have a personal relationship with Christ. I'm trying to express to him what it means to be a Christian."

"How do you think that's going, Kim?" she questioned.

"Not too well, so far," I lamented. "He just doesn't seem to understand that Christianity is a personal relationship with Jesus, not just going to church and living by rules and rituals. To tell you the truth, it's been kind of exasperating. He's such a great guy. I just wish we shared the same faith."

My frustration mounted over time as Paul continued to turn a deaf ear to my explanation of God's place in my life. I sincerely cared about him and didn't want to give up the relationship, but his lack of interest in spiritual matters was disappointing.

One evening, my mother asked if she could share some Scripture with me. Would I be open to hearing and considering some things

I may not have thought about? I'm a pretty open person and was curious about what she might say, so I agreed.

"Kim," she asked, "I'm wondering about something. Are you planning to marry a Christian when the time comes for you to be married?" (She likes the direct approach).

"Of course I am, Mom!" I quickly replied.

"Well," she continued, "have you considered that people eventually marry someone they date? You know, Kim, couples have two choices. Either they break up or they marry. I know that you have developed a close relationship with Paul, but since he's not interested in pursuing the Lord, have you considered that you might not be in God's will in this kind of relationship?"

Ouch, she wasn't mincing any words. I listened respectfully, so she went on. "Would you be willing to listen to some Scriptures about God's desire regarding relationships?"

I agreed to listen.

She plunged right in. "I Kings 11:1-4 talks about how Solomon had loved many foreign women. By foreign women, God meant pagan women who did not follow the true God. He told Solomon not to be involved with them. Did you know there was a compassionate reason why God took such an adamant stand on that subject?"

Hmmm, I had never thought about that. My curiosity was peaked. What could that have to do with compassion? "No, Mom, I guess I need further understanding."

With that, she went on to read from I Kings. *"For they will surely turn your heart away after their gods. Solomon held fast to these in love.... For it came about when Solomon was old, his wives turned his heart away after other gods; and his heart was not wholly devoted to the Lord his God...."*

"Kim, God spoke to Solomon and warned him not to be involved with women outside his faith, that things could get complicated. Solomon ignored God's words and soon his heart turned away from Him. I don't want that to happen to you. God didn't warn Solomon not to marry women of other faiths just to be mean. He had his best interest at heart. God always wants what is best for us. He saw the future and wanted to spare Solomon the heartache that often comes when a believer marries an unbeliever. That's compassion. God sees that the danger for you in dating a non-Christian in a serious relationship is that you might eventually be drawn away from faith. I know you wouldn't want that."

I continued to listen, but by now, my heart was sinking. I could sense God convicting me, but I was also thinking of the cost of giving up Paul. I wanted him in my life.

My mom is relentless and passionate when it comes to the Bible. I knew she loved me and was sharing her heart, but I have to admit, it was hard to hear what came next.

"Let's look at II Corinthians 6:14-15, Kim." We turned to those verses and read *"Do not be bound together with unbelievers.... what has a believer in common with an unbeliever?"*

Mom talked about the wisdom of the Bible in telling us that believers and unbelievers have nothing in common spiritually. "While a couple may share many common interests...sports, friends, books, movies, etc, without the freedom to communicate a core value of Christ at a heart level, it could eventually affect their relationship. God's desire is for marriage relationships to have a strong spiritual foundation based on Him. In fact, the spiritual part of a relationship is the most important component of marriage. Kim, Paul expressed to you that He feels no need for a personal relationship with Jesus. Now, don't get me wrong, he's a nice guy. He comes from a fine family and seems to have good character, but when it comes to spiritual matters, what do you have in common? God has a wonderful plan for your future. Refraining from being bound together with unbelievers is part of that plan."

By now, I was wrestling with many thoughts. As I contemplated what the Bible said, I have to confess, it was all pretty agonizing to hear. I really cared about Paul and wanted to be with him. The thought of breaking up broke my heart and I knew it would break his as well.

Mom spoke softly, "You know how Dad and I feel about this issue, Kim, but we feel it is important that you make your own decision. Would you be willing to consider trusting God with your dating? As long as you choose to exclusively date a non-Christian, your eyes may not be open to any eligible Christian boys. I'm not asking you for an answer today, but I'd like to ask you to pray and consider making a commitment to God to date only Christians and see what God will do? Would you be willing to take some time to seek God's will in this matter?"

I sighed, feeling dejected and disheartened to say the least. The thought of breaking up with Paul was agonizing. "I will think and pray about it, Mom," was all I could offer.

Then, my emotions seemed to rise up, and I unleashed a proclamation. "But I will probably never have another date again. There just aren't any Christian boys in our town that I would want to go out with!"

With that, our conversation ended. I spent a lot of time praying the next couple of weeks, vacillating back and forth. Life with Paul versus life without Paul. I'm sure my mom was praying too. I stepped up my witnessing tactics. Surely, Paul would see the light and want to change. Sadly, my ploy was unsuccessful. I kept weighing my options. This was such a difficult and painful decision. From my teenage viewpoint, this was a nightmare.

Finally, one evening I joined Mom in the kitchen as she was cooking dinner. "I've made a decision. I broke up with Paul tonight, and I've decided to make that commitment to date only Christians."

I was resigned to the idea that I would probably never have another date. Yet, I knew my decision was the right thing to do.

"Oh, by the way, Mom, I want you to know that I didn't make my decision just to please you. God spoke to me, and I'm doing this in obedience to Him."

A difficult decision for Kim, for sure, but that wasn't the end of the story.

Reflection

First, let's reflect on some components of how God worked in this situation. How did God speak to Kim? He spoke to her heart through Scriptures that held biblical principles. When Kim heard verses explaining God's reasons for not dating outside her faith, it began to resonate in her heart. She could have resisted His word, but she allowed it to take root and begin to grow. As she prayed, she realized, difficult as it was, she had to make a choice. Gradually, her thinking changed. Her heart was tender, and her relationship with God was ultimately more important to her than her relationship with Paul.

There's more to this story, and I think you'll find it interesting. God not only heard Kim's commitment but honored it in a very special way. About two weeks later, we were having a youth group meeting in our home. The doorbell rang, and when I answered it, there stood a young man I had not met. He turned out to be a friend of our pastor's son who lived in a nearby town. He had come up to Sturgis from Indiana to see what was going on in our Michigan youth group. I introduced myself to John, a very nice looking, tall, blond, blue-eyed teenager. It quickly became clear that he was a strong, committed Christian. He and Kim soon began to date with our wholehearted approval. John and Kim later became engaged in college and then married.

At their engagement party, his family and ours gathered to celebrate with a dinner in our home. After serving dessert, I said I had something to share with everyone. "John, I want you to know that I have been praying for you since you were about two years old. We had recently become Christians, and I had begun praying for Kim's future husband. Over the years I added things that I hoped for in Kim's future spouse. My list grew to include many attributes. John, I want you to know that you are the answer to every prayer I have prayed for Kim's future husband over the past twenty years."

With peaked interest, John's mother, Carolyn, asked what I had prayed. "Well, I prayed that Kim's future husband would be brought up in a Christian home and that he would accept the Lord at an early age. I prayed he would have a love for people and a passion for God and the Bible. Among other things, I also asked God to give him a servant's heart and that he would be a man of character."

Sharing a smile with Carolyn, I reaffirmed, "Like I said, John, you are the answer to my prayers."

God's word is truth and when we allow His word to speak into our lives, we walk in the place of blessing. Kim heard the logos (written word of God) as I read Scripture to her that night long ago when she was in high school. The Holy Spirit then quickened it to her heart, and it became a rhema (personal word) to her. She chose to respond, which put her in the place of blessing, and she found God could be trusted to provide an amazing Christian man for her after all. John has been a faithful, godly husband who has brought much joy to Kim's life for twenty-five years, including five wonderful children.

A personal word from God and heeding that word literally changed the course of Kim's life. Indeed, the cost of her decision in high school was great. Some words are easy to hear and easily followed. This one, for Kim, had a higher cost, that of leaving someone she truly cared for with no promise of what her future would hold. But I have to ponder as to how her family would have turned out if she had chosen another course in life. Would she have been able to freely raise her children to love the Lord? Would her children have been conflicted concerning spiritual matters? Would Kim's spirituality have caused a wedge in her marriage? All powerful, pensive questions that I'm thankful never had to be addressed.

As Bill and I have reflected on Kim's decision, Bill sums it up well by saying, "It's wonderful to have your children listen to you, but it's even more exciting when they are tuned in to the Lord, seeking His heart in a matter. In all honesty, they probably listen better when the Lord speaks to them personally. I have to believe that it blesses the Lord when his children come to Him with their needs. Looking back on this story twenty-five years later, we still see the fruit. Not only is Kim's family wonderful, but there is fruit in their children as they learn to also take their needs to the Lord, listening to and depending on Him in their lives. Watching two generations beyond ours seek His wisdom is a special blessing as we grow older. I think this is the hope of every parent and grandparent in Christ."

Class Reunion

In this next story, you will see the power of God's word illustrated in a decision I had to make about attending my 30th high school reunion. Living a great distance from Johnstown, Pennsylvania, where I grew up, I had not visited any of my high school friends in thirty years. Anguish and misery describe my memories of that period in my life. Targeted in those formative years as an object of taunting and mocking, I was convinced that I was both inferior and unattractive. High school was not a happy time for me, and even the thought of returning for more abuse was distressing.

In the thirty years that had passed, I had come into a personal relationship with Jesus Christ and had walked with the Lord for the previous twenty years. Many past wounds had healed. I felt like a whole person, but gnawing at my soul was an unanswered question. Would I be a whole person if I were around my high school peers again? In some ways, I was curious about returning to my past, but in other ways, fear gripped me. Would I be opening myself to more pain?

As I prayed about whether to go, I sought a settling word from the Lord. *Lord, will You give me some Scripture that will help me know if it is Your will for me to attend this reunion?*

My reading was in Isaiah that day. Immediately, a section from chapter fifty-one caught my attention. *"Look to the rock from which you were hewn, and to the quarry from which you were dug."* My spirit quickened as I began to sense God nudging me to go back to the place I had come from, to Johnstown, to that quarry where I'd grown up, that place from which I was first carved out.

Reading further, the Lord continued to encourage, comfort, and reassure me that He was leading me to go to the reunion. In verse three, I read, *"Indeed, the Lord will comfort Zion; He will comfort all her waste places. And her wilderness He will make like Eden, and her desert like the garden of the Lord; Joy and gladness will be found in her, thanksgiving and sound of a melody."*

Pondering these words, I saw that this verse described my high school experience, one of waste places, wilderness, and desert. Yet, a promise was present in the verse that God would comfort, that He would make those places a garden. My confidence began to grow, and I decided that I would attend the reunion by faith. God had spoken a very special word of encouragement and reassurance to me. I would stand on those words. I had no idea what I would encounter at the reunion, but I knew God would be with me. Little did I know that I was in for an amazing surprise.

The day finally arrived. We had driven from Michigan to Pennsylvania the day before and checked into a lovely hotel downtown. Although a bit nervous, with God's personal word sealed in my heart, I was able to walk into the reunion with strength and assurance. As I entered the dining room of the country club where the reunion was held, all my old fears melted as people greeted me with enthusiasm and embraced me in friendship. No one bullied me, teased me, or gave me strange looks. It was almost surreal. My heart was warmed as they seemed to want to talk with me, were even happy to see me. In fact, I felt honored when classmates who had been popular opened a place for us at their table. Was this really happening? Because of their kindness, conversation was easy and flowing. It was a wonderful evening, far beyond my expectations.

What I had been blind to was that my high school acquaintances had grown and matured over the years, too. They had put away childish behavior and were acting like caring adults. With bondage to my past broken, we all enjoyed a fabulous evening. With no anxiety, I experienced a security that only the Lord could provide.

Bill's words later expressed it well, "Betsy, I felt like I watched God heal your inner memories right before my eyes."

Just as God had spoken a garden into my desert, as expressed in the ancient text of Isaiah, so He fulfilled the rest of the verse. Joy and gladness overflowed in my heart along with thanksgiving and the sound of melody. I'm so thankful God spoke His words of support and comfort to me *before* I went to the reunion. How insecure and fearful I would have been otherwise, but He chose to bless me and bring closure to a thorny and complicated past.

I guess that is one of the Lord's specialties, renewing people. II Corinthians 5:17 expresses it this way, *"Therefore if anyone is in Christ, he is a new creature; the old things passed away; behold, new things have come."*

Expose Yourself to Scripture

One thing is evident. If we want the Lord to speak to us through the Bible, we need to expose ourselves to God's Word. God desires that we know His Word, meditate on it and learn to walk in it. He longs to speak to us personally through Scripture. The God of the Bible is a relational being who loves connecting with His children. By submitting ourselves to the teachings of the Bible and listening for His voice, we are sure to hear Him.

Several passages, mostly from Psalm 119, speak specifically to the importance of knowing the written word of God:

> Psalm 119:105 - *"Thy word is a lamp to my feet, and a light to my path."*

> Psalm 119:92 - *"If Thy law had not been my delight, then I would have perished in my affliction."*

> Psalm 119:71- *"It is good for me that I was afflicted, that I may learn Thy statutes."*

> Psalm 119:11 - *"Thy word I have treasured in my heart that I may not sin against Thee."*

> Psalm 119:9 - *"How can a young man keep his way pure? By keeping it according to Thy word."*

Psalm 119:18 - *"Open my eyes, that I may behold wonderful things from Thy law."*

Psalm 85:8 - *"I will hear what God will say; for He will speak peace to His people, to His godly ones...."*

Matthew 4:4 says, *"...Man shall not live on bread alone, but on every word that proceeds out of the mouth of God"*

When we in America think of bread today, we think of it as part of a meal. We don't count bread as the most important aspect of any meal. However, that was not the case in biblical times. To them, bread supplied a main staple of their diet, not a side item. Their bread contained high value in nutrition and nourishment.

Yet, considering the benefit and significance of bread to first century believers, God declared that it wasn't enough. Something else also merited attention. Something else existed which needed to be added for wholeness and health. The element to be added held such great significance, such high value, that to be without it diminished quality of life and potentially threatened spiritual health. The implication was clear. Spiritually, we can't live without a word from God. *"...Man shall not live on bread alone, but on every word that proceeds out of the mouth of God"*

"Word," in this verse, is interpreted from the Greek word rhema, a personal word from God. God intends for us to live by the rhema that He speaks into our lives. He never intended for us to exist on physical bread alone. We are so much more than just a physical being. Our physical body is the housing for our soul and spirit. In the Bible, we are referred to as a temple in which God is to reside. As such, we desperately need the feeding of spiritual food, His Word, as well. By design, God has made us to live on every personal word He feeds into our soul. This constitutes our spiritual nourishment and is as necessary for well-being as our physical food.

To guard against spiritual malnutrition, God wants us to feed on rhema words specifically designed for our individual needs. God's generous provision allows us to be spiritually healthy.

In order for the Scripture to become personal to us, we must spend time in it. Then, when a situation arises where we need a specific word from God, we will have a well of living truth to tap into. The Holy Spirit will draw on the resources hidden in our heart and speak Scripture back to us. God invites us to hear His voice. Our part is to listen.

God's Love

Scripture is a great way to hear God's voice, whether for peace, blessing or assurance. However, God also uses His Word to speak practical lessons into our lives. I'm sure you have stories of your own. Hopefully, mine will remind you of them.

As a new Christian, I remember the first time I was aware of God speaking a personal word to me through the Bible. A missionary was visiting in our home, and as we talked one evening, she turned to me and said, "Betsy, I have a verse I'd like to share with you that has meant a lot to me over the years." She flipped through the pages of her Bible until she came to a verse in Isaiah. As she read it to me, something in my heart cried out. *Yes, that is exactly what I need to hear. Thank you so much. This verse changes everything.*

I bet you are wondering what that verse was. First, let me give you a little background. I grew up in a church-going home. My parents were good people, but to my knowledge we never heard the gospel message spoken in our church. Even though we were very involved in church programs and activities, none of us had a personal relationship with Jesus Christ.

When I was in high school, an evangelist came to our church. It was the first time my father heard the gospel message, and he accepted the Lord that night. Thereafter, he became zealous for the Lord and often quoted the Bible to us. I had not attended the meeting and was definitely not interested in his newfound religion…AT ALL. Whatever he may have shared with me landed on a closed heart.

Years passed. I graduated from the University of Kansas, met my future husband, Bill, and married. We moved to Oklahoma where our two girls, Kim and Laurie, were born. A couple years later, Bill's work moved us to California. It was there, at 26 years of age, that I *heard* the message of salvation for the first time. Maybe I had heard it before, but I don't recall it or had tuned it out. Finally, my father's prayers were answered, and I embraced the Lord with all my heart. I was so thankful to finally have real meaning and purpose to my life, to know that life was more than just chasing after the next fun moment.

Because of events from my past, like all who come to Christ, I was a broken person who longed for someone to love me with unconditional love. So, when my missionary friend read Isaiah 43:4 that night in our home, it washed over my soul like the refreshment of a warm cup of tea on a cold wintry day. Maybe God will speak to you through this verse too. God was speaking, and the part of the verse that grabbed me was *"Since you are precious in My sight, since you are honored and I love you…."*

God knew exactly what my heart longed for. I needed for Him to tell me personally that He loved me, that I was special to Him. And there it was. Later I looked up the meaning of each of the words in the verse. *Precious* means to be of great value, costly, and dear. *Honored* means highly esteemed, well regarded, and greatly respected. *Loved* means strong affection, to take pleasure in, to delight in.

As I pondered these meanings, I allowed my soul to absorb them deep within. I realized that God saw me as a person of great value. He highly esteemed me. He took pleasure in me and delighted in me. It was humbling to realize that God did not define me by my shortcomings and weaknesses but loved me just because He created me.

That night, as God redefined to me who I am, I began to become rooted, grounded and established in His love (Eph. 3:17). After that, times when I asked Him if He had anything to say to me, He frequently told me again who I am and what I mean to Him. Now that's freedom!

My prayer is that it will become a common experience in your life to hear God's voice and to know how much He loves you. Not just words on a paper, but deep in your heart, that He will give you affirming verses just as He did for me. May the love of God keep your heart and mind in Christ Jesus.

Preparing to Move, Again!

Let's look at more experiences when God spoke through Scriptures. When Bill was offered a promotion to move to his company's home office in Michigan, he considered the change and all it would involve for our family. Living in California, we had become accustomed to modern buildings, progressive thinking, beautiful, new neighborhoods, a church we loved, and of course…malls in close proximity.

Contemplating a move to a small town in Michigan, Bill admitted that the words "older, farming, rural, and manufacturing" best described our new location when compared with California. Not that these were bad, just different from what we were used to. Questions loomed in his mind. Did he want to move his family to such a completely different lifestyle, from bustling, suburban California to a small, quiet, mid-western farm community? Would we adjust? It would definitely be radically different from what we knew in a more metropolitan environment. Basically, we would be going from an area with over six million people to a small town of ten thousand.

Even weather would be a factor in our adjustment. Our southern California climate was sunny and warm most days. Michigan had extremes in weather, everything from hot, humid summers to frigid, snowy winters.

Beyond that consideration, Bill felt apprehensive about his new position. In sales management, there had been a lot of freedom with his time at his discretion. Meetings with customers and salesmen were outside the confines of an office. He now faced a nine to five office job. A schedule that lacked flexibility could be stifling. What adjustments would accompany this change?

Several other issues also weighed on his heart. First, his company was in the process of being taken over by another company. Would it be a friendly take-over? Second, they had promised to buy our house if we couldn't sell it, but their offer was thousands of dollars lower than our asking price. This didn't sit right. Finally, although the company offered Bill a higher position, the raise seemed inadequate. With all these questions, the burden of the decision for his family's future weighed heavily on his mind. He knew he needed to hear from God.

Restless, and unable to sleep one night, he decided to spend time with the Lord. Should he move his family? Was it God's will? His mind wrestled with the decision late into the night.

Opening his Bible, he began to read Psalm 37:3-5. The words seemed to leap from the page, so fitting for his situation. *"Trust in the Lord and do good; Dwell in the land and cultivate faithfulness. Delight yourself in the Lord; and He will give you the desires of your heart. Commit your way to the Lord, Trust also in Him, and He will do it."*

Many times, Bill had read these familiar verses in the course of daily Bible reading, but this time proved different. It was as though God took a yellow highlighter and marked these particular verses as they spoke directly to what he was struggling with. Upon reading God's rhema, peace flooded his soul. He knew he had heard from God. He had his answer.

The Lord revealed that day that he should trust Him in this move. God showed him the bigger picture. He was to dwell in Michigan with the purpose of cultivating God's faithfulness in himself as well as in others. God revealed He could be trusted to give Bill the desires of his heart as he delighted in Him. As Bill committed his way to the Lord, he sensed God would go ahead of him, prepare the way, and accomplish His plan.

In just a few moments, this personal word from the Lord through Scripture changed the state of Bill's heart from an unsettled predicament to calm assurance. This is the way God often works and demonstrates the power of a rhema word. The words Bill read from Psalm 37 evidenced more than just words on paper imprinted with ink. Charged with the power of the Holy Spirit, they became living words capable of filling Bill with peace and renewed direction.

I'm reminded of Hebrews 4:12. *"For the word of God is living and active and sharper than any two-edged sword, and piercing as far as the division of soul and spirit, of both joints and marrow, and able to judge the thoughts and intentions of the heart."*

God's word became a living essence for Bill that night. It cut right through the issue he was grappling with and ministered a soothing answer to his dilemma.

We made the move to Michigan, and Bill found satisfaction in his new job. Although his position in the company was Product Manager, he also, beyond his job description, contributed a number of innovative ideas to the company, even inventing many new products which greatly benefited the company financially. He very much enjoyed the satisfaction of creativity in the workplace.

We have been part of several churches in Michigan over the years, and in each one Bill has added value through his teaching, leadership and mentoring skills. Truly, he has *"lived in the land and cultivated faithfulness."*

Apostle John's Observation's Regarding Trials

Bill and I both enjoy teaching the Bible. What we love most is when God reveals something fresh to us from His Word, just as he did with Bill the night he wrestled about a move. As we read along in Scripture in preparation for a lesson, often a particular verse will stand out. It's almost like the text will radiate a special light. A rhema word is especially helpful when we're going through a trial. Some time ago, God revealed a special secret to me regarding the problems and troubles we have in life. I don't have any particular trial in mind right now, but just want to show again how God can disclose truth through Scripture, perhaps as preparation for future trials. The secret appears in a number of verses, but we will look at a few as a teaching.

Revelation 1:9 is the verse I'll start with. *"I, John, your brother and fellow partaker in the tribulation and kingdom and perseverance which are in Jesus, was on the island called Patmos because of the word of God and the testimony of Jesus."*

There are many angles to studying this verse, but what God had me focus on were the words *tribulation, kingdom, and perseverance.* I like to look up the meanings of words, so that was my starting place with this verse. In my concordance, I read that *tribulation* means anguish, burden, persecution, trouble, affliction, a sense of being crowded, and suffering. I especially relate to the idea of 'a sense of being crowded.' It's true that when we're in a time of trial, we often feel crowded or squeezed in, trapped by the events that are taking place.

Next, I did a word study on *perseverance.* It was defined as patiently suffering, cheerful or hopeful endurance, to stay under, to undergo or bear trials with a sense of expectancy. The cheerful part struck me as odd at first. Who considers it a cheerful matter to endure suffering? I usually picture a person who perseveres as one with a brooding expression, struggling to stay the course while being bombarded by various obstacles. I do not picture a cheerful countenance. Yet, when I looked up the word *cheerful* in Greek, interestingly, it is the word 'hilaros.' Do you see what I immediately saw? That word looks amazingly like our English word 'hilarious.' This means cheerful endurance, not just with a hint of a smile but with extreme joy, merriment, and a positive outlook. There must be a secret, I thought, as to how this is possible. How can a person in the midst of a trial appear as happy as one who has just won the lottery? God was only too eager to impart the secret to me.

I saw that John considered himself a 'fellow partaker' of anguished suffering while feeling crowded in his troubles. Surely, being banished to the island of Patmos, he felt just that. But in the midst of his trial, he chose to persevere. He was able to suffer cheerfully because he was hopeful. He expected to see God's hand in the midst of where he found himself. His faith was strong.

God revealed to me that the reason John could cheerfully endure, had everything to do with the third word in the verse, *kingdom*. The word that appears right between tribulation and perseverance in Revelation 1:9 is *kingdom*. How interesting, but what does *kingdom* mean? *Kingdom* means to rule or reign. It denotes royalty, the foundation of power and authority.

A light bulb went on in my thinking as God spoke to me the reason John was able to persevere expectantly and even cheerfully through his trial was because He understood kingdom. He recognized the value of Christ's rule and reign in his life. He was keenly aware of and appreciated that Jesus, the very foundation of all power and authority, would empower him to endure his tribulation. He did not have to endure his difficulty in his own strength or by his own might. He was alert to God being right in the center, balancing the trial with perseverance. Kingdom made all the difference in John's expectation for the future. He could even be cheerful, as the definition suggests, because he knew who was ultimately in control of his life, the One who not only knew the outcome, but who also promised a future and a hope.

God's rhema word to me regarding the secret to suffering with grace impacted my life. As I taught this concept to others, perhaps they too experienced a fresh way to look at their trials.

Rejoicing in Trials

Another section of Scripture that God used as a personal word to me regarding trials was Habakkuk 3:17-18. *"Though the fig tree should not blossom and there be no fruit on the vines, though the yield of the olive should fail and the fields produce no food, though the flock should be cut off from the fold and there be no cattle in the stalls, yet I will exult in the Lord, I will rejoice in the God of my salvation."*

Surely, if there was any time in the Bible that sounds like an occasion of suffering, this was it. The experience of Habakkuk resonates as one of wilderness and emptiness, a barren time of drought. Nothing was going right. The trees were not blossoming nor were they bearing fruit. The crop had basically failed, producing no food. The flocks were also cut off, and the cattle were gone. From the description, this seemed like a time of defeat and despair.

What is significant about this passage is the response of the writer. If anyone should be in sack cloth and ashes, crying his eyes out, it is the person enduring this trial. But look at how he reacts. He makes an intentional choice to *exult in the Lord*. By an act of his will, he *rejoices in the God of his salvation*.

Again, a word study was in order. I found that the word *exult* means to rejoice, make merry, boast, crow, brag, or bluster as opposed to bewailing, mourning, sorrowing, grieving, lamenting, bemoaning, and crying.

This man, who had a complete crop failure and lost his livestock, did not choose to bemoan his bad luck. He did not wail in misery. No, he made a choice to rejoice to the point of blustering and bragging in God.

But that's not all. *Rejoice,* in this verse, means to celebrate with violent emotion, clamorous jubilation to the point of looking foolish. Can you picture this? We have a man who has lost his crop and his cattle but who is jumping up and down, loudly and raucously rejoicing before the Lord. Does this even make sense? Picture him in your mind's eye. Picture yourself in the same or similar situation.

Maybe your trial isn't loss of crops or cattle. Maybe your test has to do with sickness, grief, financial problems, or relational difficulties. Whatever your ordeal, what is God looking for as a response?

This was a huge rhema word to me. Perhaps it is to you, too. This man understood *kingdom* in the midst of his trial. He had taken Revelation 1:9 a step further. He was rejoicing.

What is it that Habakkuk understood, that we sometimes miss? I think the answer lies in verse 19 when he says: "*The Lord God is my strength, and He has made my feet like hinds' feet, and makes me walk on my high places."* *Hinds feet* symbolizes sure footed confidence. Habakkuk understood that the Lord alone would strengthen him in the midst of his trial. His confidence in God's ability to carry him through the trial was unwavering. His faith was unshakable. He truly believed God.

In the midst of tribulation, Habukkuk saw that it was God who made him walk on his high places. High places were locations chosen as places of worship, places where an altar to the Lord was present. Habukkuk realized it was God who had positioned him at the place of worship. He knew that the moment insurmountable circumstances surrounded him, they were actually an invitation from God to enter into the sacrifice of praise and rejoicing. Have you ever considered your trials as an invitation to praise God, to worship Him with abandon, to rejoice in Him?

Thinking of trials with this new mindset brought a refreshing freedom and purpose to my own difficult times. I often feel helpless in the midst of a trial, but this novel perspective renewed my thinking, brought a measure of anticipation, and even meaning to the hardships of life. It's comforting to know that God's intent is to build our endurance through trials and hardship.

When Habukkuk 3 was partnered with Psalm 27:5-6, it seemed to round out my understanding of the principle God was endeavoring to disclose. *"For in the day of trouble He will conceal me in His tabernacle; in the secret place of His tent He will hide me; He will lift me up on a rock. And now my head will be lifted up above my enemies around me, and I will offer in His tent sacrifices with shouts of joy; I will sing, yes, I will sing praises to the Lord."* It would seem that David also grasped the secret of enduring the trials he encountered. He, too, understood kingdom.

I would challenge you to consider applying these truths to the next trial you find yourself facing. If you have never rejoiced during a trial, it will seem odd at first. It may even seem foolish. But what have you got to lose? It is possible you may tap into an unexplored approach to your future problems. Let this be a rhema word that takes root in your soul as well. Go ahead. Give it a try.

Study Guide 3

1. When God speaks to us, what kind of changes can we expect in our lives?

2. Can you share a time when God specifically spoke to you through the Scriptures?

3. A. If we want God to speak to us through the Scriptures, what one thing is essential?
   B. Meditate on Psalm 103 or 118 and ask God to speak to you.

   1) Write down any verse, word, or phrase that jumps out.

   2) Ask God how it applies to your life.

4. Discuss the importance of the word from each of these verses.
   A. Psalm 119:105
   B. Psalm 119:92
   C. Psalm 119:71
   D. Psalm 119:11
   E. Psalm 119:9
   F. Psalm 119:18

5. Discuss the meaning of Matthew 4:4 in light of spiritual nutrition.

6. Did anything stand out to you as you read about *trials, kingdom, and perseverance*?

CHAPTER 4

God Speaks During Prayer

> *"Call to Me and I will answer you..." (Jer. 33:3).*

The Prayer of Release

How often have you found yourself in a situation beyond your control, one you wrestled with and spent yourself on solutions that just didn't work? At the end of your rope and without resources, you began to sense a quiet nudge from God to seek Him in prayer. Not just any prayer, but the prayer of release.

You may ask, "What is the prayer of release?" This powerful prayer is one that lies at the very center of God's will. Jesus taught the disciples to pray this way when He said, *"Thy kingdom come, thy will be done..."* (Matt. 6:10). Jesus, Himself, prayed a prayer of release on His way to the cross, *"...Father, if Thou art willing, remove this cup from Me; yet not My will, but Thine be done"* (Lk. 22:42).

To pray this way means that we are willing to submit ourselves and the concerns of our lives to the Lord. In essence, we give up our right to run our own life. Doesn't it make sense that if He is the Lord, then decisions should be His? By definition, Lord means ruler, the one in control. Our issue becomes one of trusting Him as the authority in our lives. Although Jesus wants to be Lord of everything in our lives, the prayer of release most often comes to our attention when we have no more options and no idea how to proceed.

Whether we call on God with the prayer of release at the beginning of a trial or later, it is distinguished by two important steps. First, we completely surrender the troubling matter to the Lord, giving him full rule over it. This may take some time to do as it requires a genuine shift in thinking, a shift where we take our hands off the problem and give it to Jesus. I find it interesting that this concept appears in verses referencing worship. Psalm 63:4 *"So I will bless You as long as I live; I will **lift up my hands** in Your name."* Lifting up our hands denotes a posture of surrender. When our hands are lifted, we cannot easily defend ourselves.

Once a concern is released to God through prayer, then we must step back and trust Him for an answer. As you can imagine, this requires faith. It is a prayer that calls us to let go. This, of course, is one of the most challenging components of the Christian faith.

Obviously, this should be our heart's desire with all of our problems. Often, however, we go through a long journey of frustration and anguish before we come to the point of relinquishing situations to the Lord. Finally, at our rope's end, out of resources, and with nowhere else to turn, pale and weak, we completely turn the difficulty over to Him. Blessed is the person who can release a situation without trudging through the mire of anxiety first.

When we hear God calling us to pray the prayer of release, and we submit to Him, it frees the Lord to adjust either our thinking or our situation. The choice of change is completely up to Him since He now owns the problem. Staying close to Him in prayer is always wise, but especially critical at these times.

There have been times when the Lord has spoken to me by directing me to pray the prayer of release. The results have varied, but the Lord has always been eager to take control when that prayer has been offered. Let me show you how this has worked for me.

Set Me in Large Borders

When our family moved from California to Michigan, there were many adjustments to be made. I remembered my mother's advice when she used to tell me, "Betsy, in life, there is nothing more constant than change." Yes, there were many changes on our horizon. We moved to the Midwest in January from a warm, sunny climate to cold, overcast, snowy weather. It snowed heavily on the bitterly cold January day we moved in. Blizzard winds continued to blow all that first week, closing the schools. "Snow Days" were something new to us but very much pleased our girls.

With newly purchased coats, sweaters, mittens, scarves, hats, and boots, a snow shovel, and a snow plow (Bill's first purchase), we Californians forged our way into our new arctic like conditions. The weather was so cold, the furnace didn't turn off until May. Yes, really. In fact, because of huge snowfalls, we didn't see the ground until late April that first year.

I recalled the last words one of my California friends said as she bemoaned our move. "If I ever moved back to the Midwest," she said, "I'd probably spend winters with my nose pressed against the window, tears streaming down my face." When she spoke those words, I found them amusing and thought, *That will never happen to me because I feel positive about our move.*

On top of adjusting to the never-ending cold, shortly after moving, I discovered I was pregnant with a late in life baby. A surprise at first, that involved revised planning, we all quickly looked on this turn of events as a joy.

Our home in Southern California had not sold due to a recession in the housing market, so we rented a small house in Michigan. Our hope was to move into a more permanent home soon. *Surely this arrangement is only temporary*, I thought as I looked around the tight quarters that would serve as our residence.

"Oh, well, we can be happy here for a couple of months," I told Bill. Neither of us thought it would be any longer than that. But God had other plans.

Time passed, days turned into months with no sign of selling our California home or of buying one in Michigan. Discouragement began to knock on the door of my heart. Little things started to bother me as we continued life in the rental house. The ice cold, frost-covered dishes, taken from cupboards on walls lacking insulation, had to be warmed in the oven before meals. The carpet was beyond cleaning and reminded me of greasy hair. Old linoleum in the kitchen never looked fresh, never sparkled, and the bathroom tub defied my scrubbing, always looking dull and grimy. Some of the upstairs walls even had mold growing on them. As I walked the rooms over creaky, drafty floors, the days seemed ceaselessly gray and bleak. The consistent below freezing weather left me chilled to the bone even when wearing layers of heavy sweaters. Sometimes, I felt so cold, I wore my coat indoors.

Being pregnant, morning sickness was also my constant companion. I seemed to tire easily and felt more emotional. All these changes, plus supporting Bill and the girls in the move, left me exhausted.

I felt myself sinking, my mood as gloomy as the weather. Stuck inside, behind closed doors, with no friends and not much to occupy my time, *Oh, woe is me* soon became my mantra. It wasn't long before I found myself sighing, just as my California friend had predicted, nose pressed against the window, tears rolling down my cold cheeks. *Oh for a day of sunshine; oh for a larger house; oh for new cupboards, fresh smells, a shiny kitchen floor.* My list of miseries went on as my mind crept toward depression. Some days, it was as though I were shaking my finger in God's face and admonishing, *I don't like this, Lord. I don't like this situation one bit.*

Spring came late. The first tulips and daffodils, although beautiful to my color starved eyes, were soon covered with a late snow. Easter pictures were taken outside, the girls shivering in their new Easter attire and quickly running back into the house for what warmth they could find. I had to laugh, though, when I spotted a dainty, yellow daffodil peeking up through a snow drift in the yard. *So, this is spring in Michigan!*

One morning, as I awakened, it dawned on me that I needed to do something about the state of my soul. Even I was getting tired of my own complaining and the wretched state of my mind. I'm certain my self-absorption was affecting my family too. They would surely appreciate some relief. Frankly, my attitude was pathetic, but, alas, what could I do to pull out of my unhealthy frame of mind?

After sending the girls off to school one morning, I settled on the couch, a blanket tucked securely around me, and began to read Psalm 118. For some reason, I felt more focused that morning, and the Lord gently reminded me of something I had definitely lost sight of. *"Give thanks to the Lord for He is good..."* (Ps. 118:1).

I was brought up short as I read those words. *Oh, my goodness, He's right. I have not been thankful for a very long time.* I had been so focused on how miserable I perceived my circumstances that thankfulness had completely eluded me.

For the next few days, I pondered that thought, that distinct word from God, and began a half-hearted effort to give thanks. My attempt, however, could only be described as feeble and rather pitiful at first as my heart was not fully engaged. But as I continued to practice thanks each day, a slow, if not awkward change began to be birthed in my heart. As I spoke gratitude to God for things I was sincerely thankful for, a loving husband, happy children, health, and a baby on the way, He began to speak to me about releasing the house situation to Him, the very circumstance that had plunged me close to despair. In my heart, I could hear God asking me to let go of the house, that is, to loosen my grip on the idea that I could never be happy in that house. He wanted me to give this dilemma to Him.

I persisted in thankfulness in coming days, but it took some time to bring myself to cooperate by praying the prayer of release. Days passed as my soul wrestled with God over this. A power struggle for control surfaced where I would give the house issue to Him and in the next breath take it back, repeatedly, giving it up and then taking it back.

After several weeks of waffling, teetering on the edge of decision, but never really making it, I finally made the choice to get off the merry-go-round and pray the prayer of release with sincerity. That day, I relinquished to the Lord all my hopes and dreams of another house. *Lord, I am willing to stay in this house, with all its disrepair, the rest of my life if that would please you. Not my will, but Thine be done. I will choose to accept my life and its surroundings just as they are with no expectation of change. In fact, if it would please you, I am willing to live in a hut with a mud floor.*

I will admit that would have been a stretch, but at the time that statement best described the dramatic change of heart God was bringing about in me as he encouraged me in prayer. Sincerely praying the prayer of release didn't come easily. It took some time to come to the point of allowing God to have control without taking the problem back.

How often do we give the Lord a problem and then retrieve it again the next day or even the next hour? With the prayer of release, I finally stopped the reclaiming process and permanently transferred my problem into God's hands. Each time I felt tempted to take it back after that, I reminded myself of the prayer and stood on firm ground that God had taken over management of this situation. By faith, I knew he was perfectly capable of handling it Himself without my interference.

During that time, words from Psalm 118:5 leaped from the page into my heart. They were perfect for my dilemma. *"From my distress I called upon the Lord; the Lord answered me and set me in a large place."* Elated with the idea of a *large place*, my hope soared as I wondered if God was promising me a large house. However, after reflecting on this verse, I began to see that He had already set me in a *large place*. In the past few weeks, I had not only moved into a thankful, positive attitude, but had also released the housing situation to the Lord. My soul now resided in large borders, no longer cramped by my own self will.

Each day I continued to renew the prayer of release. Because of the freedom and joy in knowing God was in control, His ways grew in my heart. Prayer is so much more than us asking for things. It's also God speaking to us. It is relationship. God knew just what I needed to hear.

Negative thinking, I recognized, is narrow and restricting. "Faith" thinking is large, spacious, knowing no bounds. It is creative, far sighted, and hopeful. Thankfulness can be a catalyst to help transform our thinking into something more positive.

Interestingly, within two weeks of my prayer of release, our California house sold, and we contracted to build a new home in Michigan. Bill reminded me of II Chronicles 20:20, *"...put your trust in the Lord and you will be established...."* Building a new home was an extra blessing. God had already set me in a large place.

Giving Up Expectations

God wants our will. When we first come to the Lord, we realize that we need to get off the throne of our life and acknowledge that position is rightfully His. We no longer control our lives, Jesus does. That is what the Lordship of Christ is all about, but it has to be worked out by daily choices. With each situation that arises in life, we have the option of who will be in control, the Lord or us. Jesus is gentle, full of grace and mercy, eager to help us walk by the Spirit.

When we offer the prayer of release to Him, we are expressing that He still maintains His rightful place on the throne of our lives. *"...Thy kingdom come, Thy will be done..."* (Lk.11:2 KJV). Not my will, but Thine. We give up our expectations of how best to resolve a problem or what step we should take next. Releasing the problem completely to the Lord, we allow Him the freedom to handle matters any way He pleases. We back off from control, yet walk by faith and move out as He leads.

When I complained to the Lord about all the things I disliked about the rental property, I quenched the Holy Spirit. In essence, my grumbling could be likened to shaking my finger at God and saying, *I'm not content with what you've chosen to provide for me.* This attitude bound God from moving on my behalf.

When I insisted God answer my prayers, my demands were met with silence. God seemed remote and unapproachable, and I grew weary. A turning point came when I surrendered to the possibility of what I feared most. Resisting God and insisting on fulfillment of my expectations actually limited me from experiencing God's best. It left me shackled to the problem.

On the other hand, the prayer of release liberated me to receive God's solution. It unleashed the creative power of Jesus, my Master. If we believe that nothing comes into our lives unless first sifted through God's hands, then we also must believe He can not only handle our problems, but He also wants to. We can know that His answers will always be better than ours.

Source of Anxiety

Anxiety is everywhere today. Who doesn't know someone who lives daily with anxious thoughts? Maybe, it's you. Anxiety is often accompanied with a number of physical and emotional symptoms: fear, tension, muscle tightness, headaches, digestive disorders, ulcers, back aches. The list goes on.

Why do we experience anxiety in our lives? Often it is because we realize we cannot resolve a problem on our own, but we're not sure we can trust God to solve it either. We want peace, but we have trouble believing God will really come through with an adequate answer. With our limited knowledge, we are blind to the understanding that God may have a creative answer that we have not yet considered.

Our natural tendency is to cling to our problems, not wanting to give up control. Yet the Bible tells us, *"And why do you call me, 'Lord, Lord,' and do not do what I say"* (Lk. 6:46)? If we call Him Lord, then shouldn't we allow Him to act as Lord over our problems? The Bible tells us to be anxious for nothing, to make our requests known to God, and then experience His peace in the matter (Phil. 4:6). Yet, anxiety seems to ride on the coattail of problems. We long for peace as we're moving through a trial, but instead, fear and apprehension become our companions.

There is a human tendency to want to be "problem solvers." After all, God gave us minds to think, the ability to solve issues, to discover solutions, but it is easy to slip away from acknowledging God by moving into a flesh centered solution which ends in frustration and anxiety. Romans 13:14 exhorts us to *"make no provision for the flesh."*

There is a way, however, to disarm and dismantle anxiety, frustration, and even fear. We can find it through the prayer of release. As we relinquish situations to the Lord, in time, we begin to sense peace. We may not have a resolution to the problem immediately, but a deep inner confidence begins to well up as we understand that God is in control. Fear cannot stand in the face of the reality of God's loving Lordship.

This is all a process. It involves daily dying to self and choosing to walk by faith. It takes making the decision to trust God, then daily seeking Him, calling on His strength and trusting His promises.

Sometimes, at this point, God answers the prayer. Often, a knowing comes that God has taken control, and with that, a sense of peace washes over us. Perhaps a Scripture comes alive, and we receive a word from the Lord, or an attitude may begin to soften and change. Relinquishment can be the first step of what God wants to do. God called me to pray the prayer of release regarding our house in Michigan. He changed my heart first, and then He moved in the situation.

Unidentified Sickness

Many years ago, God also asked me to pray the prayer of release during an extended illness. To this day, it remains unidentified, a mystery to me and the medical community. What I do know is that this ailment had put me in a state of great discomfort. Not knowing what was wrong, I visited a doctor who decided that I had an infection and sent me home with an antibiotic. After taking the allotted dose, I returned to the doctor still feeling ill. He prescribed another antibiotic, and then another, until I had been on medication for six months with no results. Many tests followed and along with them, puzzled doctors. Nothing concrete could be determined, no firm diagnosis established. Bouncing from a dermatologist to a gynecologist to an endocrinologist, I ended back with my general practitioner.

When he decided to send me to another specialist, I realized I had come full circle. In my panic and frustration, it began to dawn on me that no one in the world had ever heard of my symptoms. Neither had anyone ever treated a case like mine. My illness had the medical profession stymied and that thought left me feeling utterly helpless and powerless. Terribly frightened, I had a foreboding awareness that no doctor could restore me to health. I prayed often about this ailment, sometimes crying out to God, *I cannot accept this; the unknown is too frightening.*

In my desperation, I came to the point that I didn't care what the doctors found, I just prayed they would find something. I remember sitting in one doctor's office looking into a microscope with him. Searching for a parasite or another foreign creature from a culture he had taken, I all but willed one to appear. I insisted the doctor prescribe medicine just in case I had this or that disease, but it all proved for naught.

As the pain and discomfort continued, I became an emotional wreck. *Why, God, why won't you take this ailment away? I can't function anymore.* I pleaded with God.

For two years, I searched for help, praying and appealing to God to heal me. Nothing changed. It seemed as though God had abandoned me, leaving me to my own resources.

Finally, one day I heard that still, small voice gently whispering to me that the road to peace would come when I accepted the ailment. That was truly a remote thought. How could I accept it? After all, isn't God a healer? The Lord reminded me of Proverbs 3:5-6, *"Trust in the Lord with all your heart, and do not lean on your own understanding. In all your ways acknowledge Him, and He will make your paths straight."*

Truth be told, if anyone had ever spent time leaning on their own understanding, it had been me during those two years. Fretting and worrying thrived as the fruit of my own understanding. Like most people, I like to control what I can, but this lingering ailment had me boxed in with no ability to manage it. My inner resources had left me emotionally bankrupt. Broken and without resources, I knew I had to respond again to God's call to the prayer of release and acceptance. After much angst, at the end of my rope, I whispered the pray He was waiting for.

Lord, I accept this affliction. I don't know what it is, but you do. I am willing to be in a state of discomfort the rest of my life if that will please you and bring glory to your name. I accept whatever you want to do with me. I belong to you - your will be done.

At that moment, a thought struck me that I recognized as a personal, rhema word from the Lord. He challenged me with the thought that I had not really recognized Jesus as Lord of this affliction. I had sought healing but not the Lord Himself and had found no peace in seeking my desire to be well. Peace is only in Jesus and seeking after Him. Do you see the difference? We can seek a solution, or we can seek the Lord. I had been seeking a solution. As I released myself to the Lord and recognized His Lordship over the ailment, God's peace began to rest in me for the first time in two years. My trust was now in the name of the Lord, no longer in healing. My health belonged to Him. I assured myself that what He chose to do would ultimately be for my good. After all, isn't that the essence of faith?

The next two weeks nothing changed physically. Pain and discomfort persisted, but my soul looked to the Lord and continued to reaffirm my commitment of release and acceptance. While still experiencing pain, I had peace.

Then one Sunday, our church had a healing service. Sensing God wanted me to go forward, I received prayer and anointing with oil and asked God to heal me. While acknowledging that I wanted His will to be done, I submitted myself again to acceptance and release. My eyes focused on Jesus, not on a healing. My trust continued to be in the Lord, not in recovery. Being just where God wanted me, at that moment, God graciously began to restore my body to health.

In retrospect, there never has been a diagnosis, and I still have occasional minor bouts with the issue, but God has given me ways to manage the mild pain, and I know He is with me. I think of Psalm 23:4, "*...Thy rod and thy staff comfort me.*" The presence of the Lord was enough to comfort me. I sometimes wonder how much my heightened state of anxiety actually contributed to and exacerbated that illness.

Reflection

Not every ailment we have will be completely resolved in this life, but that does not negate God's desire for us to submit our problems to Him. Paul carried a thorn in his flesh for many years. Still, God gained glory in the midst of the trial he endured, and his trial was used to teach him dependence. In the same way, much of our character and faith is both built and strengthened through our trials.

God had spoken personally to me about what it meant to submit to Him. He had brought me to the point of praying the prayer of release and acceptance. This freed the Holy Spirit to heal if He chose to. My anxiety and worry had boxed me into such a state of tension that I had quenched the Spirit, but God responded to my heart of trust. He waited for me to come to the end of myself and my resources and to rely wholly on Him.

Sometimes God heals through the hands of a doctor, other times He chooses to miraculously heal. Still, other times, healing doesn't come in this life. There is no one method or answer for every case. The key is prayerful submission to Him so that He can personally weave His will into our lives.

When God calls us to the prayer of release, our hearts focus upon the Lord because He alone is our hope and our help. Our faith is in the Lord, not in what we want done. God's plans for a situation may be different than ours. When we release our condition to him, He is free to fulfill His purposes.

I wonder how many of God's plans for our lives remain on hold because we're busy shaking a finger at the Lord telling Him, *I don't like this; I won't accept this; I can't bear this.* Relinquishing control aligns us with God's intent.

Daniela from Czechoslovakia

When Bill and I visited Czechoslovakia, we stayed in the apartment of a lady named Daniela. A delightful Christian woman, she began to tell us about her life.

"My husband has left me," she lamented. "I want so badly for him to come back. I have four children to raise and we need him here."

As we prayed throughout our stay with her, one evening she asked us if God had spoken to us concerning whether her husband would ever return. We told her we hadn't received any word to that end. Discerning that she had placed all her hope in yearning for her husband, we felt led to impart to her the benefit of the prayer of release. In her case, this prayer could lead her to lay aside the worry, fretting and anxiety she was experiencing and bring her into a refreshing freedom and peace of mind.

"Daniela," I began, "we are so sorry that your marriage hasn't worked out. Of course, it is God's will for marriages to stay together, but your husband has chosen to leave, and we know how difficult it has been for you to accept that. That kind of rejection is never easy, but maybe God wants a shift in your thinking about this situation."

Daniel looked puzzled but interested to hear more. "Your hope has been focused on reuniting with your husband. Your heart is broken. Yet, as you go through this trial, this is an opportunity for you to redirect your hope so that it's in God alone, not in the hope that the divorce proceedings stop."

We asked her if she would consider releasing her husband to God and trust Him regardless of what that might involve. Would she give God permission to control this event in her life?

We continued to gently speak to her, "Sadly, your husband may or may not choose to return, Daniela. If your only hope is in your marriage, you may be setting yourself up for disappointment, but you won't be disappointed by placing your hope in the Lord. Let Jesus be Lord in this situation. Let Him be the One who orchestrates your life in the midst of your marital crisis. Let's release this setback to Him and allow Him to deal with your heart and your husband's decision according to His will."

Daniela saw the wisdom of this approach and chose to release her husband as we prayed together. She began to accept her situation that night as trust in God prevailed. Several months passed and we received a letter with this testimony in close to perfect English. "I have accepted that I am not to set hopes on our marriage being restored, but that it is the Lord alone who must be and can be my only hope - the Lord alone, not 'the Lord who will save our marriage.' Either He will deliver us out of this now, or even if He does not, His name must still be blessed for the marvelous promise of Romans 8:28 still holds with the word 'all.' How wonderfully liberating!"

Daniela was referring to Romans 8:28, *"And we know that God causes **all** things to work together for good to those who love God, to those who are called according to His purpose."*

Another verse that aptly described her choice is I Timothy 6:6, *"But godliness actually is a means of great gain when accompanied by contentment."* Daniela had moved her heart into a position of contentment and rest.

I lost track of Daniela over time, but in her last letter, she had moved from continual anxiety to abiding peace. Why? Because God spoke to her and she had experienced the power of the prayer of acceptance and release.

Seventeen Problems

Prayer is such an integral part of our Christian walk, yet how many times do we approach God with an issue that needs attention and really expect to hear an answer? How often is that our first response? Sometimes things build up in our lives, and we become overwhelmed.

In the following story, you will see how God was not only intimately acquainted with all my ways but had a plan He delighted to reveal.

Several months after we settled into our home in Southern California, I experienced a nagging sense of frustration. Feeling emotionally fragmented, I noticed stress and exasperation were my constant companions.

One morning, I awoke almost immobilized by these overwhelming feelings and thoughts. *What's bothering me, Lord? I'm feeling frustrated, but I can't put my finger on why? Will you reveal to me what is wrong?*

I had asked the Lord a question in prayer. Now by faith, I awaited His answer. Several Scriptures tell us that God delights in answering our prayers. *"...if you shall ask the Father for anything, He will give it to you in My name. Until now you have asked for nothing in My name; ask, and you will receive, that your joy may be made full"* (Jn. 16:23-24).

The Lord's answer may not be immediate, but in time, He will reveal an answer when we seek Him in prayer. Jeremiah 29:12-13 contains a wonderful promise. *"Then you will call upon Me and come and pray to Me, and I will listen to you. You will seek Me and find Me when you search for Me with all your heart."*

Having brooded over my mood for several weeks, I asked God to show me what was bothering me. For some reason, I could not figure it out. I just knew that something was stealing my peace. Maybe you have had this experience, where you know something is out of kilter, but you can't quite put your finger on exactly what it is. With pen and paper in hand, I listed the things that floated across my mind. My list gradually unfolded to reveal a number of issues as I engaged in *listening prayer* and heard God's voice.

In our newly built home, the yard was still just dirt, and I wanted grass. Completion of the pool lagged behind schedule. We had not found a piano teacher for the girls. No gutters were on the house yet. Friends for the girls proved sparse. We needed new furniture for the family room. I had no Bible study group to attend.

Determined to continue hearing from God about what bothered me, I remained still, waiting on the Lord, and listening further. The woeful list went on: No letters from home, no rapport with new neighbors, no ministry, no ongoing creative projects. No, no, no....

Perusing the list, I counted seventeen unsettling things in all. I was gaining a clear picture of why I felt frustrated. It wasn't just one thing. It was seventeen. Being an analytical person, I began to categorize the list which revealed five items concerning the house, six involving the girls, and three miscellaneous issues.

God is a God of order. He had first helped me arrange and catalog areas of frustration into a pattern. That, by itself, eased my mind. Next, He revealed that ten areas were beyond my control. Action could, however, be taken on the remaining seven.

Seventeen items had robbed my peace. Focused time with the Lord, listening to Him in prayer provided a word of knowledge. My next step involved more prayer. In that prayer time, I released the seventeen obstacles to God. Then I asked for grace to accept the things I couldn't change and wisdom to handle the areas that could be changed.

After several weeks, I looked again at the list. To my delight, eight items could be marked as done. I wrote TYL (thank you, Lord) beside each of these. After six months, I again revisited the list and happily crossed off all the remaining obstacles. *"This poor man cried and the Lord heard him, and saved him out of all his troubles"* (Ps. 34:6). Ah, yes...that described me!

God loves to hear from His children in prayer and to respond to our needs. I've noticed that it is often the little things that mount up in life that have the potential to rob me of peace. Maybe, it is the same for you. Muddled and confused, I sought counsel from God. He spoke specifically, even revealing to me what bothered me. Then, He directed me through steps leading to renewed peace and contentment.

Did God Speak to Biblical People During Prayer?

How common is it for God to speak to people during times of prayer? Do we have a record of God speaking to any people in the Bible while they were praying? Yes, this frequently happened.

In I Samuel 23:10-12, David, anxious about his safety, inquired of God about Saul's plans to pursue him. God replied with a specific word that Saul was coming and the men of the city were planning to surrender him to Saul. This word of knowledge from God during a time of prayer spared David's life.

When we pray, we need to practice waiting for the Lord's answer. It is so easy to ask God a question, then go on to the next thing, without waiting for an answer. What if David hadn't waited for God's reply? What if he petitioned God in prayer and then went about his work without listening for an answer? His life might not have been spared. God never meant for our communication with Him to be a monologue. It is meant to be a dialogue. He is a communicator, and one vehicle He uses to communicate is prayer. He wants to play an active role in our prayer life, not a passive one. Prayer is not simply talking to God; it is talking with Him.

We usually think we understand our part in prayer. We talk to God, tell Him about things on our heart and send up requests. But God also has a major role in prayer. He listens, and He speaks. Through practice, we can develop spiritual ears to also listen. His response has the potential to change our lives.

Moses, in Numbers 21:7-9, interceded in prayer concerning the sin of the people. Showing their impatience with God and Moses, the embittered Israelites complained and grumbled against them. Later, as the people confessed their sin, Moses prayed for them, and the Lord began to speak to Moses. He gave him instructions that anyone bitten by a snake should look to the bronze serpent, and he would live. If Moses had not listened for God's voice during his time of prayer, many Israelites would have needlessly died.

Again in Acts 10:9-16, Peter went to a housetop to pray. While praying he received a vision. Then the Lord spoke to him, *"And a voice came to him, 'Arise Peter, kill and eat!'"* Peter recognized it as the Lord's voice. A second time, the Lord spoke saying, *"...What God has cleansed, no longer consider unholy."* During his time of prayer, Peter heard from God. As he listened, God's words arrested him and changed his thinking in a crucial area. As a result, he recognized that God accepted Gentiles as well as Jews. There are many other people in the Bible who heard God's voice in prayer, but from these few, we have established that God does use prayer to relate to people. Sometimes, He gives a fresh perspective as we seek Him in the midst of a trial.

College Dilemma

In this next story, through prayer, God showed me clearly what to believe. What an amazing outcome as we walked by faith. It was October of 2001. Although our son, Mike, had been accepted into the college of his choice with a very nice endowed scholarship, he had opted to take his first two years at our local junior college. They had awarded him a full ride Presidential Scholarship which he decided to accept. He was resolute in his decision as he reasoned he could get his first two years of college free and only have to pay for the last two. It made sense.

However, six weeks into his classes, he felt he had made a huge mistake and longed to be away at the larger school. Disappointment grew with each day. Living at home without the full experience of college began to seem like two more years of high school.

Easy to solve, I thought. We'll just phone the out of town college he now wanted to attend, tell them about the dilemma, and enroll him the next semester with their promised scholarship. It turned out not to be as easy a transition as I had thought. How surprised I was with their response. I did not see coming what happened next.

"Oh, we are so sorry," the admissions counselor explained to me, "that scholarship was only good if your son joined us at the beginning of his freshman semester."

Stunned, I hung up the phone and moaned, *Oh, no...we're too late. We've really blown it. The scholarship is lost.*

Over the next week, I prayed about the situation and decided to phone the college a second time. Again, I asked if there was any way the scholarship could be reinstated. "No, we are sorry, but this is our policy." It was a closed case.

I continued to pray, *God, there must be a way.* Almost immediately my mind heard words from Matthew 19:26, *"With man it's impossible, but with God all things are possible."* These words startled me because they were the opposite of what the college was saying. *Lord, how can this be? The college has said it is impossible.* But the words were repeated again in my mind. *"...with God all things are possible."*

These words felt so powerful that faith began to rise in my heart. I had no idea how, but God was going to somehow open a way for Mike to attend this school with the scholarship. Something in me knew it. Beyond rational reasoning, I was completely convinced I had heard God and that He was about to give Mike his heart's desire.

Paul, at one time in II Corinthians 11:23 said, *"...I speak as if insane...."* I understood his sentiments exactly, especially as our situation was about to get worse.

As I spoke with the college a third time, I received the same message. "Mike is welcome to enroll in school next semester," the admissions counselor said, "but we can't see our way clear to offer financial help. Our policy stands that if you don't start as a freshman, you lose the entire four years of scholarship money. You can't come in as a transfer student and receive the scholarship. We are so sorry."

For them, it was a matter of school integrity, and they needed to be consistent. For us that amounted to a $24,000 loss.

Back to prayer. Once again, I began to earnestly seek God. The exhortation that *all things were possible with God* grew in my heart, and soon I felt that this school was where God wanted Mike to be, and that God, in His supernatural power, would somehow make it happen. The firm *no* from the college had become a small obstacle in my mind compared to the firmer *yes* I was hearing from God.

Persistence became my middle name. We decided to try once more. This time Bill, Mike, and I made an appointment and traveled to the college to talk with admissions in person. I'm certain they were puzzled to see us, but they were very professional and kind.

As we sat in the waiting room, Mike was called in by himself for a conference. After fifteen minutes, the admissions counselor left but asked Bill and I to come in with Mike. Mike was downcast as he related the same doleful news we had heard on the phone. The admissions counselor had confirmed the worst. The rule stood. The situation looked hopeless. But God....

"Mike, I don't understand it, but somehow all things are possible with God," I stated with assurance.

The next 15 minutes dragged by slowly as we waited for the administrators to return. We prayed together once more. Soon the admissions counselor returned to the room accompanied by the Vice President of Admissions. We were surprised to see a broad smile on her face and wondered why she was so happy all of a sudden.

"I have talked with the Vice President of Admissions," she related, "and we have found a way for you to receive the scholarship, Mike." My heart leapt. God was at work. We looked at each other with renewed hope and expectancy.

The Vice President approached us and explained. "We have come up with a way Mike can receive the scholarship while still maintaining the integrity of our scholarship policy."

We were all ears, waiting to hear how they had resolved this seemingly impossible problem. "Since our policy is that a student only qualifies for the scholarship if he is a first semester freshmen, we can offer it to Mike if he is willing to drop out of junior college now, without finishing his semester there. Then he could come to our school next semester as a first semester freshman. We would have to reinstate his application, and then we could honor the scholarship that we previously offered him."

By now, we were all beaming with excitement, thanking God for his amazing provision, but there was more to come.

The administrator continued. "Not only will we offer him the previous scholarship, but because of Mike's extensive high school Spanish, we feel he could begin with Spanish 4. If he can maintain a "B" average in that class, we will "give" him twelve credit hours for Spanish 1, 2, and 3 without charge and without taking those classes."

We were stunned by their generosity. Basically, beyond the reinstated scholarship, they were offering Mike a free semester with no study or cost. Since Mike planned to minor in Spanish, this was truly an unexpected bonus. When God decides to bless, He often does it in abundance, more than we can ask or think. We were amazed by His grace and provision.

When we arrived home, Mike, immediately and happily, dropped out of the junior college. He found a job and spent the rest of that semester working. The next semester he enrolled at the new college and went on to graduate in three and a half years. While he had missed a semester by starting his freshmen year late, he actually gained it back with the Spanish offer. This enabled him to graduate with his class. Our God is an awesome God, truly a God of the impossible, a God of fresh starts. God hears our prayers and delights in responding to us.

A Reversal of Destiny

Hearing God's voice as we pray can apply to any situation. While God faithfully spoke to me as I prayed regarding Mike's quest for a school scholarship, in this next narrative, you will see God's faithfulness in a time of dire physical illness. Often, it is in times of distress that we especially need to hear His voice. For me, it was loud and clear.

It was a Saturday in early May of 2004, just a few days before Mother's Day. Finally, the sun shone brightly in Michigan, a long awaited reprieve from another harsh winter. Busily weeding and planting a spring garden, I had not brought my cell phone outside with me. Bill was gone for the morning, having traveled about thirty miles to a nearby town for a business appointment. Mid-morning, as

I busied myself in the garden, the ringing phone in the house did not reach my ears.

Finishing my chores, I later went into the house and checked for phone messages. One from Cindy, a friend in a nearby town, put me on edge. "Call me right away, Betsy. Bill is here and seems quite sick."

Cindy lived in Constantine, about half an hour from our home in Sturgis. Bill's appointment had been in Jones, Michigan. Occasionally, Bill would drop in to see Cindy's family on his way home from a job. We had been close friends for years.

I wonder what's wrong with Bill. He seemed fine when he left this morning, I mused.

Immediately, I phoned Cindy while re-planning my day, which now most likely included picking up Bill. "Betsy, Bill came by our house and seems very sick. We are all concerned about him. He has thrown up a lot and seems disoriented. Can you come get him?"

Mildly alarmed, I put a few things together and headed out. I asked our pastor to ride along so he could drive Bill's car home. Upon arrival at Cindy's, I found Bill sick in the bathroom and suffering from what he thought was a terrible migraine headache. This seemed odd because about ten years prior, God had permanently healed him of migraines, and he had not had one since. Prior to the healing, his migraines had been so serious that a number of times he had to come home from work to recuperate. We thought that was in the past because one night Bill had been sitting in front of the TV watching the 700 Club when Pat Robertson said he felt God was healing someone with migraines. Bill actually had a migraine as he watched, so he put his hand on the TV as Pat prayed. Instantly, he was healed and had not had one since. This was truly a miraculous answer to prayer.

Now he was complaining, not only of a headache, but of difficulty with his vision as well. Helping him into the car, we started our trip home with frequent stops along the roadside as he continued to be sick to his stomach.

At home, still puzzled as to what was wrong, we decided he should go to bed and sleep it off. Two hours later, he was up, somewhat confused, and emotional.

"Something's not right. I think we should go to the hospital," he groaned. So, I helped him to the car and drove to our hospital emergency room.

We explained to the receiving nurse that Bill was having a migraine. She strapped the blood pressure cuff on his arm, and we both watched the numbers rise. As the numbers clicked back down, she looked me in the eye and soberly declared, "He is not having a migraine."

Scurrying him to X-ray, before I had a chance to assimilate her declaration, they slid Bill into a CAT scan unit. I stood nearby watching the screen as the lab tech scanned Bill's brain.

"What's that big white spot on his brain?" I innocently asked.

"The doctor will explain," the technician said with sympathy in his eyes.

Increasingly, I felt I knew what it was. My stomach roiled as I fought back tears. Bill was having a stroke, and I was looking at a mass of pooled blood in his brain. Until now, I had not expected a stroke was the issue since he did not have the normal symptoms of a drooping face, slurred speech, and weakness in an arm. Now, the doctor confirmed my fears.

"Bill has had what we call a hemorrhagic stroke," he explained. "This is where the blood vessel doesn't actually burst, but the pressure is so great that blood seeps through the vessel into the brain. His was behind one of his eyes."

Before I had a chance to process what was happening, Bill was whisked into a helicopter headed for a larger hospital an hour away in Kalamazoo, one which specializes in stroke victims. Meanwhile, after tearful phone calls to our children, I phoned friends who quickly responded by coming to drive me to the hospital.

Upon arrival, they settled Bill into the neuro-intensive care ward and started a fluid drip in his arm. That was all. Surprisingly, the doctor seemed laid back and basically did nothing for him. With such a relaxed, if not apathetic, response from the doctor, I wondered what the rush had been to get Bill to Kalamazoo. With increasing concern, I asked why no tests were scheduled until morning. "How do you know the bleeding isn't increasing as we speak," I asked in alarm.

His answer was numbing. With a disturbing calmness, he looked me in the eye and stoically replied, "If it was increasing, he would be dead."

I was stunned, but had no further questions at that time.

The morning tests revealed no additional bleeding in his brain. We now had to wait out many days as the doctor attempted to stabilize his continually vacillating blood pressure. No surgery could correct the problem, I was told, so none was performed. The damage to his brain remained to be seen. I was only allowed to see him a few minutes each day. Family joined me in the waiting room for the next 10 days. And so we waited....and prayed.

When Bill began to normalize, they allowed longer visiting time. Early in his hospital stay, I noticed Bill seemed to be having visual difficulties. Wondering how bad it was, on one occasion, I came into the room and stood quietly about a foot from his face. When he didn't respond, the nurse said, "Bill, look who is here."

Turning his head this way and that, he queried, "Who?" He was scanning the room and could not see me right in front of him. A dreaded thought hit me. *My husband was blind.*

Pumped with morphine and other drugs, Bill seemed oblivious to the gravity of his situation, but emotions swirled in my mind and heart. Would I be taking a blind man home? What changes would that require? Could I do this alone? What should I expect? Feeling overwhelmed, I turned to the only place I knew to turn, to God. As I interceded and appealed to God for Bill's sight, a thought welled up in my mind, a thought I knew without a doubt was God speaking to me. *Call a prayer meeting together, Betsy, and cry out to Me for Bill's sight.*

I emailed many friends that night, and we all gathered the following morning to passionately pursue God for Bill's healing. Intensely praying many Scriptures over Bill's situation with much zeal and fervor, we were not going to *have not* because we *asked not*. We stormed heaven with persistent, persevering prayer. I knew this was Bill's only chance to see again. We needed God to move on his behalf.

A couple days passed with more waiting and more prayer. By then, he had been blind for over a week. Then one day when I walked into his hospital room, he announced, "It looks like it's raining out today."

Pausing, I turned and took in the meaning of those words. "Bill," I questioned with hesitation, "how do you know it's raining?"

Well, I see it out the window," he replied as though I must have a problem.

"You can see it?" I inquired.

"Yes, of course," he replied.

Needless to say, I was rejoicing as I realized anew the awesome power of prayer. We have a God who hears and answers prayer, One who speaks words to build faith, who spoke to me to call a prayer meeting on Bill's behalf and then honored our prayers by restoring Bill's sight. Nothing is too difficult for God. Not only was there an answer to prayer, but God Himself was the one who initiated prayer in the first place by nudging me to call the church to pray. He is a mighty and loving God who even foresees our needs.

Bill's recovery was lengthy, but his sight continued to improve until only a small bit of lower left peripheral vision was lacking. Today, he is able to drive with no problem. Through therapy, he learned to write again, and after much practice was able to do math problems as well. With continued prayer, today no one would guess he ever had a stroke. Many look at him as a walking miracle.

About a month after the stroke, our son, Mike, was visiting with Bill and asked him, "Dad, how are you really doing?" Bill's immediate response brought tears to Mike's eyes.

"Mike, I am the most blessed man on earth. I have so much to be thankful for."

Mike will never forget his father's response, one of thankfulness in the midst of one of life's biggest trials. We do have much to be grateful for. Our family has seen God's direct answer to prayer many times, but this was the most powerful one. It's been a reminder to find things to be thankful for every day.

In the summer of 2009, Bill celebrated his 70th birthday. All year I planned for this joyful occasion with much anticipation. To me, it was a miracle that after five years, he was still alive. Quite a milestone, but now we are looking forward to 2014 when we will again celebrate. This time, his 75th birthday, ten years after his stroke. Indeed, we are thankful.

Study Guide 4

1. What do you expect from God when you pray?

2. Read John 16:23-24 and explain what that means to you personally.

3. A. What is the prayer of release?
    B. Did any of the stories on prayer of release resonate with you? How?
    C. Have you used this prayer? Explain.

4. How did these biblical people hear from God while praying?
    A. Numbers 21:7-9
    B. Acts 10:9-16
    C. I Sam. 23:10-12

5. Look up II Chronicles 20:4-30
    A. What was the essence of the prayer in this section?

    B. What was the Lord's answer, the rhema word from the Lord?

    C. What was the outcome that showed God's power was in His word to them?

6. Share a time you have received a rhema word while praying.

7. Can you say in your heart that nothing is impossible with God? If not, ask Him to reveal Himself to you.

CHAPTER 5

God Speaks Through Circumstances

"Your ears will hear a word behind you,
'This is the way, walk in it...'" (Isa.30:21).

Camping in the Rain

F OR THOSE OF you who are campers, have you ever noticed that camping and rain are synonymous? Bill and I are camping groupies. I have to include at least one tale of camping in this book because it has been such an important part of our family life for many years.

When our children were small, we spent many vacations in forests and mountains, around campfires, and on hiking trails. We had converted our Volkswagen van, or bus, as they were called in those days, into a mini camper of sorts. With the back seats out, a double mattress fit nicely, making a bed for Bill and me. Each night, we stretched a homemade cot above the two front seats for our younger daughter and then placed another small mattress across the back, over the motor, for our older daughter. It was very snug, but it worked well.

We also stretched a piece of canvas outside the door of the van, propping it up with tent poles. Although it sagged in the middle, it kept us dry as we went in and out during rain storms.

On this particular trip, it had rained continually for three days. You might have guessed, yes, we were in Oregon where rain is typical. Often, when it rained, we would continue our travels, all the while trying to stay in a good mood. But after three days in the van, continually soggy, the dreariness of the weather was stealing my joy. With growing edginess, all of our tempers were short. It was becoming harder to keep a good attitude. We needed to get outside of our cramped quarters, even if for only a few hours, but the continual patter of rain kept us inside.

Finally, on the third night, we tucked the girls in bed, listened to the plunkety plunk of the dripping on the roof and eventually drifted off to sleep. In the middle of the night, I awoke having to use the restroom. Groggily, I slipped on Bill's cowboy boots and adjusted my poncho over my pajamas. Fortunately, it was dark so the other campers could not see my ridiculous costume. I have no doubt I was a sight to behold.

Just as I was about to exit the camper, I heard a dreaded sound, one that no camping parent wants to hear...the sound of a child throwing up all over her cot. I maneuvered out the door of the camper, groaning at the obvious mess I would now have to clean up. Irritated and angry, I made a quick turn toward the van's front passenger door. In so doing, my head bumped the canvas stretched across the side. Of course, it was filled with rain water. As it jiggled a bit, the overflowing tarp proceeded to dump gallons of water onto my head.

By now, everyone was awake, laughing hysterically at their mother standing in oversized cowboy boots, pajamas, and poncho, drenched from head to toe. At first, the scene did not seem at all funny to me, but as the girls laughed with glee, the tension and discomfort of three days trapped inside the van suddenly released. I began laughing too. We all helped clean up the various messes and finally settled in for the rest of the night.

I have always remembered that camping story because it represents life. Here is what God later revealed to me about that incident. Sometimes, the difficulties of life can cause us to feel trapped in small, enclosed places. Then, something out of the ordinary happens, and you can't help but laugh.

The Bible says in Job 8:21, *"He will yet fill your mouth with laughter and your lips with shouting."* I like to think that it was the Lord who filled our mouths with laughter that night. *"A merry heart does good, like medicine"* (Prov. 17:22). Yes, our laughter was good, and as laughter so often does, it gave a fresh perspective.

Highway Trouble

One of the things I hope to do through this book is to expand our thinking, so that we will come to recognize that God is interested in every aspect of our lives, both the tragic and the laughable events. He longs for us to be aware of His presence in every situation we encounter. Not only does God speak through the Scriptures and during prayer, but He also speaks to us through life circumstances. The following is one of those experiences in California when God made Himself known in a special way.

Traveling home from another family vacation, we cruised along the highway in our aforementioned, blue Volkswagen van. The girls were in the back seat as we all engaged in cheerful chatter about the relaxed, fun week we had enjoyed away from home.

Without warning, as we journeyed home on Interstate 5, a highway which runs the length of California, the van's motor suddenly locked. With lost power, our only choice now was to coast to the shoulder of the road and park. As the speedometer crept downward, we slowly crawled to a standstill on the side of the road.

With several failed attempts to restart the van, we finally realized the engine was completely dead. We were not going anywhere any time soon. So, there we sat. Our hope now was that help would come quickly. This was before cell phones, so we were stuck there until some kind person would come to our aid. Surely, this wouldn't take long as there was a solid stream of cars racing by, the van shaking with each passing vehicle.

For the first fifteen minutes, we watched cars rush by, hoping at least a police car might spot us. As scores of cars whizzed past, we soon realized it might be a long wait. No one seemed eager to assist us.

Then, a small voice began to speak to Bill and me at the same time with the same thought. We looked at each other as we both expressed what we felt the Lord was saying. *Use this time to thank Me and sing to Me.* This was not a hard request to comply with as we enjoyed praising the Lord in song. Bill had brought his guitar along on the trip, so we and our children began to sing songs of praise and thanks.

Sometimes, circumstances make our lives uncomfortable, and we tend to complain and grumble. Happily, this time we seemed to sense God was up to something. We decided to relax and not become stressed. About two hours went by. Time goes by quickly when you are busy, and we were occupied with singing. Still, no one stopped to help us. The afternoon wore on, and evening was quickly approaching. We had been praying for help to come but now decided to be more specific and ask God to send someone by six o'clock. We eagerly watched for an answer to our prayer as the time ticked by.

At exactly six o'clock, a car pulled over and agreed to contact a tow truck for us. Before long, a tow truck arrived. Tim, the driver, introduced himself, attached his tow to our vehicle and invited us to sit with him in the cab. Since it was a holiday, we knew there wouldn't be any garage service available, so our tired, but content family climbed aboard, ready for the hour and a half trip home.

Driving along, it didn't take long for us to begin to understand God's purpose for the delay in help. As the young driver began to chat with us, God's plan quickly surfaced. Without any prompting from us, Tim poured out his life story revealing many heartaches and disappointments along the way. As we listened politely to the tangled mess of his life and marriage, we realized the circumstances involved in our meeting this young man were no accident. God was at work.

If our van had not stalled, we would not have had the opportunity to meet Tim, a person who needed a reminder that there was a God who loved him and cared about the circumstances of his life. When Tim finished his woeful story, we knew the Lord had given us a divine opportunity.

"You know, Tim, we have some good news for you. Did you know that Jesus loves you and that He would welcome the chance to help untangle the difficulties in your life?"

Tim listened with interest, so we continued. "Tim, God says in the Bible that He has a plan for your life. He is the one who created you, and He is able to restore your damaged relationship with your wife. Beyond that, God is interested in healing the wounds of your heart." Tim seemed interested in what we shared with him as he listened intently, clearly absorbed in our conversation.

While we don't know what transformation took place in his life that day, we know for sure that God had purposely set up this appointment with Tim, a man who desperately needed to hear about hope for his future.

As we arrived home and said goodbye to our new friend, we recognized God had given him a glimpse of His love and an opportunity to turn his life around. Seeds had been planted. Isn't that all God asks from us?

I'm inspired by I Corinthians 3:6-7, *"I planted, Apollos watered, but God was causing the growth. So then neither the one who plants nor the one who waters is anything, but God who causes the growth."* It's so freeing to know that we are just called to plant seeds and water them. We are incapable of truly changing anyone. That is God's department. Our part is to simply share Jesus and leave the results to God. After all, He is the one with the power to change lives.

Circumstances such as this are an opportunity to listen for God's voice. It wasn't an accident that we were on that particular road and picked up by that particular tow truck. Choosing to keep our attitudes right, through thanksgiving and singing, prepared us for the opportunity to share Christ with a stranger, handpicked by God to help tow our van.

I can't help but wonder if we had given in to complaining and grumbling in the midst of our own inconvenient circumstance, would it have kept us from hearing the driver's need? Would we have then thwarted God's prompting to respond? Did heeding God's cue to sing and pray in our van actually prepare our hearts for this divine appointment? In the Psalms alone, the words, "give thanks" appear forty-four times. When the Bible repeats a theme, we can acknowledge it as an encouragement from the Lord to respond.

James 1:2-3 says, *"Consider it all joy, my brethren, when you encounter various trials, knowing that the testing of your faith produces endurance."* This is a wonderful exhortation that has come to mind in many of life's events to help me keep the right perspective. We can know that when a trial comes, God desires to produce something good in us. Because of that, we can rejoice and count it joy.

Inconvenient interruptions are a normal part of life. Much of Jesus' own ministry came out of interruptions. In part, because of our media, advertising, and worldly philosophies, the American way has been reduced to comfort and convenience, whatever is easy and expedient. However, this isn't always God's way. He has plans for us, and He determines the means whereby His plans are birthed and developed. We can quench his plans with our attitudes, or we can walk in adventure and victory as we listen for His voice. The choice is ours. After all, we are a people called to walk by faith.

Baby Saves Mother's Life

Continuing the theme of God using uncomfortable situations to bring glory to Himself, the following story is a vivid illustration of God performing an amazing work in a desperate situation involving a very sick woman. It really portrays well the truth that God can use circumstances to speak to people in order to accomplish His purposes. Sometimes His word is a simply "yes" or "no."

A number of years ago, a doctor related this unusual story in a Right to Life publication, (*Right to Life of Michigan News,*

November-December, 1987). To me, it contained a stirring message from the heart of God. Hear what God spoke through this unique set of circumstances.

Eleanor, a young wife and mother, lay dying in her hospital room. Her body, battling a continual high temperature, had wasted away to eighty-seven pounds. Eleanor had tuberculosis in the lower lobes of both lungs. Each lung had a hole that was increasing in size. Operations and other treatments were considered, but in her weakened state, they seemed inadvisable. Occasionally, she rallied enough to return home for a day or so but always ended up back in the hospital.

Months rolled by as she continued to deteriorate. Then, doctors began to notice something odd, that even without eating, she seemed nauseous. Stumped by this new and strange symptom, they decided to give her a pregnancy test, remote though the idea seemed.

To their amazement, Eleanor was pregnant. She was quickly given the option of abortion and even encouraged in that direction by the medical community. Her own life hung in the balance, she was told. Abortion seemed like a logical step to the doctors. In their thinking, there was no way the baby could survive nine months, and there was even less hope that Eleanor could survive the pregnancy in her condition.

In her heart, however, Eleanor heard a clear, "No," to the idea of abortion. She decided to carry the baby. Though carrying a child added much extra burden to her already over-taxed system, she and her husband determined to continue the pregnancy. The outcome would be in God's hands, but she knew she could not end another person's life.

The doctors must have shaken their heads at what they considered an inadvisable decision. Yet, they were compelled to do what they could for Eleanor to try to keep her alive for as long as possible. While honoring her request, the doctors nevertheless felt that Eleanor had sealed her doom. No way could her ravaged body support her life and that of a baby. By all medical standards and protocol, her condition appeared to be terminal. Because the situation seemed hopeless, none of them could have imagined what was about to happen.

About mid-pregnancy, the doctors noticed that Eleanor's temperature had dropped to normal and her color was beginning to return. Soon her appetite came back and she began to gain weight. Upon X-raying her lungs to determine the cause for this positive and unexpected change, they were stunned to discover something that went on to make medical history. Truly a miracle was taking place.

It seemed that as the baby had grown larger, his body was pressing on Eleanor's diaphragm. In so doing, the baby was accomplishing what the doctors had been unable to do. As her diaphragm compressed, the sides of the holes in her lung pushed together, thus beginning and eventually achieving a natural healing. In essence, the baby was saving the mother's life.

Eventually Eleanor delivered a healthy baby boy. Within a month, a perfect baby and a strong mother returned home. Eleanor completely recovered.

Such a story holds a powerful spiritual lesson. The baby, at first, seemed an overwhelming burden to an already weakened body. Yet, the pressure of the burden was the very instrument God used as a tool of healing and restoration.

Eleanor could have chosen to abort her baby, resulting in her own death; but she chose instead to carry her son to term. God had spoken a clear "no" to abortion.

From this story, I think a thought provoking question begs contemplation. How often do we try to abort or avoid uncomfortable situations or relationships that God has placed in our lives? Could these be the very tools God plans to use to build, restore, or heal us?

Revelation 15:2 speaks of a sea of glass mingled with fire. A sea of glass represents peace, stillness, serenity, or calm. Fire depicts a trial, difficulty, or hard time. Yet, as the two mingle, we picture peace in the midst of the fire. The peace we often long for may be in the very center of a fiery experience.

During the trials of life, we need to carefully listen for the voice of God. He may be speaking a call to put aside selfish desires, a change in attitude or behavior, more dependence on Him, or a thankful heart. The voice may not seem as explicit as reading a Scripture verse, but the message will implant itself in our hearts if we listen closely.

God can speak to us in the midst of our circumstances. Often, His first words to us are to be thankful. Beyond that, He wants us to be aware of the lessons He may be trying to teach us. As we listen, we will be able to discern His voice. Our natural tendency is to resist God when our situation becomes upsetting. Yet, this is often when God has a word that will build our inner man and conform us more to the image of Christ.

Trials Can Be for Our Good

Often, when problems or difficulties come into our lives, the first thing we want to do is rebuke them, get rid of them. If something is uncomfortable, we think, how can this be from God? Isn't my Christian life supposed to flow and be comfortable, void of suffering? However, if anything is promised in Scripture, it is suffering.

The Bible tells us not to be surprised at the fiery ordeal that comes upon us for our testing (I Pet. 4:12-13). We are called to fellowship in His sufferings and be conformed to His death. After that comes resurrection power. We'll be called at times to conform to His death by dying to our fleshly desires or negative responses. Only then will we hear how God wants us to respond. This is how we grow in our walk with the Lord. Troublesome circumstances provide an opportunity to be led by the Spirit, to hear God's voice.

Financial Matter

Some of the hardest lessons in life can involve finances. Whether we have too little or too much, dealing with financial circumstances requires a decision of attitude. I have observed that obsessing over money has little to do with being rich or poor. It is all about perception. There are people with plenty who fret over finances just as much as those who wonder where their next meal will come from. Financial strongholds can rob peace at both ends of the spectrum.

There was a time when I felt overwrought about a financial situation. We had invested heavily in some funds, and over a period of two years, we watched their value shrink as the market plummeted to new lows. We had hoped the funds would grow, but contrary to our wishes, they did not. At the time, I'm sure I spent more time in a state of anxiety than prayer. After losing a considerable amount of money, we decided to liquidate the investment.

Although we suffered heavy losses, we were glad to be rid of the funds. Our thankfulness lasted about a week, when to our surprise, the market began a rapid upward climb. Up, up, up it went. After two years in a continual downward trend, the market now soared with daily increases. With each day's report of how much money we could have been making, I grew more miserable. This sudden rise, representing lost profit for us, felt like a slap in the face. Bitterness and anger mounted, and I cringed every time I heard a glowing market report.

After several weeks of misery, I realized I needed a personal word from God. Yes, we had money to live on, but I had placed my hope for more in an unstable market. God directed me to I Timothy 6. For days, this chapter became my companion as I carefully prayed each verse. *Lord, I have brought nothing into the world, so I cannot take anything out of it either. Truly, the love of money has caused a root of evil in me. By longing for money, I have wandered away from the faith, and pierced myself with many a pang. Help me to flee from these things as your Word instructs.*

I had fallen into the trap of depending on money instead of the Lord. As a result, I suffered many pangs of resentment and bitterness. My prayer continued, but with a new focus, *Lord, forgive me and help me not to fix my hope on the uncertainty of riches, but on God. You are the One who richly supplies me with all things.*

I had to pray through I Timothy 6 often. With each prayer, I found new relief that would last until something triggered bitter feelings again, then back to the Bible and more prayer. It took several months of meditating on appropriate verses, but the truth of the Scripture eventually took root, and I came to a fresh and more balanced perspective of trusting God in financial matters.

It is so easy to fall into the trap of "the love of money". I hadn't realized this was a problem in my life, but this particular circumstance pointed it out loud and clear. God wanted to help me deal with it by recognizing my weakness in that area and learning to trust in Him. Only then would I grow stronger.

I learned that I cannot serve two masters. God is a jealous God and unwilling to share me with any idol. He helped me to regain the understanding that all of our money ultimately comes from Him. He used praying Scripture to teach me in a deeper way that He alone can be trusted to provide all our needs. In the end, my heart was in a much more confident place, assured that God would meet all our needs, just as He promises. And He has.

Ketchup Incident

Sometimes, unlike a financial crisis, circumstances that jar us are really quite simple and mundane. As I went into the garage to take out the trash one morning, the sleeve of my bathrobe caught on the doorknob. It was just enough to jerk the trash bag right out of my hand. A ketchup bottle, which lay on top of the bag, now careened to the floor. Landing with a clunk, slivers of glass flew everywhere. Barely any part of the garage escaped the infusion of glass particles and globs of the remaining ketchup.

"Oh, what a mess," I moaned aloud. "I do not need this today!"

After my initial frustration, the Lord reminded me of I Thessalonians 5:18, *"In everything give thanks; for this is God's will for you in Christ Jesus."*

My first response: *Oh, brother. I don't feel like giving thanks right now.* But, I decided to try it to see what God planned to teach me from this minor, yet annoying circumstance.

I looked around at the mess before me. Adding to the disarray of the obvious red disaster, I noticed the general, cluttered, unkempt appearance of the garage as a whole. I realized this mess at my feet actually presented an opportunity for some in depth cleaning. A job I had been putting off for weeks suddenly moved into the realm of the urgent.

Gathering the broom and dustpan, I swept out a season's worth of dirt, leaves, and whatever else had managed to collect on the garage floor. Spinning into a whirlwind of sweeping and raking, I continued to tackle the driveway, porch, and fallen pine needles in the yard.

Later in the day, upon finishing my chores, I began to reflect on a larger picture of this incident. God began to reveal a life principle to me that has become significant in my approach to problems. Here is what He spoke to my heart.

Betsy, I have a plan in all that happens to you. Sometimes, you will enter my plan or chain of events for your life by way of a calamity, suffering, or illness. In other words, life may be going along smoothly, when suddenly a ketchup bottle smashes to the floor. Abruptly, and without anticipation, an unexpected event occurs.

The Lord continued, *I have a larger plan, but to assure that the events leading to its culmination take place, you must go this route. You will find there will actually be many blessings involved along the way. Although the process must begin with an uncomfortable situation, there will be a refining of your character in the process. I know that in your way of doing things, My plan wouldn't be accomplished because My ways are higher than yours. I love you so much that I have chosen this path, which may be bumpy, to be sure you will continually draw near to me in dependence.*

In terms of all of life, obviously this ketchup incident was a minor and insignificant occurrence. Yet the lesson the Lord spoke to my heart concerning life's trials was highly significant and life changing. Trials, I learned, can be stepping stones for our welfare. As the ketchup incident drew me to thankfulness and encouraged me to clean a sadly neglected garage, so God uses all circumstances to further our progress.

Kim's Accident

It was the Christmas season, and Bill and I had decided to do something different this particular year. We opted to join our daughter, Kim, and her family on a Caribbean Cruise. It would be their first ocean cruise, and we were excited to live the adventure through their eyes. We remembered fondly our first cruise and hoped they would have the same warm memories we shared from such a novel life experience.

About a week before Christmas, we packed our bags and flew to Southern Florida where we met up with Kim and her family who had driven their RV from Indiana. We boarded the ship together. Sailing out of Miami, we headed for various ports along the ship's route. Until the last day of the cruise, it was an enjoyable, if not predictable, family vacation. On the last day, Christmas Eve day, we sailed into Cozumel, Mexico, an island off the coast of Mexico in the Atlantic Ocean. That's when trouble started.

After a fun morning shopping and browsing, Bill and I retired to the ship's deck to play cards and relax. Kim and her family chose to head out again after lunch to rent motor bikes and tour the island.

Late afternoon, Josh, our oldest grandson, back from the ride, found Bill and I still playing cards. Josh is a quiet spoken, composed young man, so when he calmly told us that Kim and Krista, his younger sister, had been in an accident, it almost didn't register at first. His manner was so cool and unruffled.

"Grandma and Grandpa, you need to come down to the ship's infirmary. Mom and Krista have been in an accident."

At first, my mind couldn't process what Josh was saying. "An accident? What kind of accident, Josh?"

"Well, Mom and Krista were riding together on a motor scooter as we traveled outside the city. Dad and I and the others were ahead of them. Apparently, Mom, in trying to keep up, came around a corner at forty-five miles per hour and lost control. She flew over the handlebars, landing on her face on the road. Krista, who shared her bike, also flew off."

As we quickly followed Josh down several flights to the ship's infirmary, we continued to quiz him. "Are they ok? What injuries did they sustain?" By now, I was feeling alarmed.

"Krista only has bruises, Grandma, but Mom was unconscious the last I saw her," Josh reported. "When Krista saw Mom on the road, she rolled her over and found her face was covered with blood. At first, she didn't think she was breathing. When she sensed the seriousness of Mom's injuries, she began yelling for help."

Josh related that an American couple pulled over in their car when they saw Kim on the road after Krista waved them down. Interestingly, they happened to have their daughter with them, and "coincidentally," she was studying to be a doctor. Upon examining the situation, she said Kim was alive but in need of medical attention. The lady's parents went on to fetch John and the others who quickly rode back to the scene. An ambulance was called, and Kim was brought back to the ship.

As we scrambled toward the infirmary, hearing all of this left us shaken and anxious. Upon arriving, we asked about Kim and were told that her injuries were severe enough that they had sent her on to the hospital. The infirmary, they explained, was not equipped to handle more serious injuries.

This was all the news we had. There was no way to know the gravity of Kim's injuries, whether she would live or die in this foreign Mexican country. Before John officially disembarked to be with Kim, he had asked the ship's Purser to have us put together a suitcase for Kim and himself. He would return to the ship shortly to retrieve it.

Quickly, Erika, our very organized oldest granddaughter, and I sped into action. Between the two of us, we had clothes, phones, and books packed, ready to go when John returned. He had no news to report so we hugged, said hasty good-byes and were now left to pray and hope.

The ship's Captain had graciously delayed leaving the port until John had retrieved the supplies we had gathered for him. It was now late afternoon and time for the ship to head out into the open seas, back to the U.S. We had no idea how bad Kim's injuries were or when we would see them again. It was a strange and disturbing feeling to depart without Kim and John. We were thankful though that we were there for the children.

As we navigated further out on the high seas, we had no communication with John back in Cozumel. We had no idea how Kim was and no way to find out. There was no phone service on the ship, and our cell phones were not only out of range but didn't work internationally. All we had was satellite internet, but we assumed John would not be near a computer. Then, we remembered Erika had packed his Smartphone which did have international service, so we quickly emailed him a message. Hopefully, we would be able to read his reply at the ship's internet café.

It was Christmas Eve. Instead of enjoying one last family dinner celebration onboard the liner, we were a pretty solemn family group, not knowing if Kim would live or die. It was a sobering night with many prayers rising to the throne of grace and many thoughts of "what if?"

We decided to skip the formal ship dinner we had all looked forward to. It wouldn't be the same without Kim and John. None of us was in a festive mood, to be sure. The girls especially loved getting dressed up, but instead, we decided to eat pizza in the cafeteria. No one was especially hungry. Our thoughts were on Kim.

After dinner, several of us decided to attend a Christmas carol sing in one of the ship lobbies. We needed a diversion to occupy our minds and pass the time. The atmosphere was quietly festive, but our thoughts were a million miles away. Laura, Josh's twin, sat with Matthew, our youngest grandson, holding him close, rubbing his back. Such loving gestures among siblings did not go unnoticed by a couple seated nearby. They later commented on the love our family had for one another. We told them the story of what was going on with their parents that night. Sympathy was extended, our pain felt by others. We appreciated their kindness in listening and caring.

Many thoughts go through your mind when you face a crisis of this magnitude. We tried not to focus on the worst scenario, but we did have to consider how we would get the children back home if Kim had to stay in Mexico for an extended time. They had driven their motor home to Florida where it awaited their return. We decided, if needed, we would cancel our flight and drive them back to Indiana where we would stay until their parents returned. It was too early to speculate how long Kim would need to stay in Mexico, but we would do whatever the situation called for. That is what families do.

We wondered what kind of treatment Kim would get. Would a Mexican hospital be up to American standards? If she had to have surgery, would it be adequate and safe? Many imaginations and plans swirled in our minds. We would only have a day to think through the situation and make decisions.

Fortunately, that evening we were able to email our other two children, Laurie, and Mike, both in Michigan. We relayed the situation to them from the internet onboard and asked for prayer. We were warmed by their speedy response and comforted knowing they would be praying.

As we reviewed various scenarios, we were reminded that Kim and John did not have passports. They weren't needed for this trip because if a ship leaves from an American port and no one stays in the country visited, you only need a birth certificate to return to America. The Purser helped us understand that it is not a problem leaving Mexico, but it would be a problem trying to return to the U.S. without a passport. Since 9/11, Homeland Security and the State Department would be tough hurdles in getting back home. "It may take weeks for that issue to be worked out," he said. We prayed it wouldn't.

Christmas morning we checked the ship's internet café frequently, hoping to hear something, anything about Kim's situation. It had been a long, restless night, not knowing. Finally, a short note from John told us what we longed to hear. Kim would live and would fully recover. Her face was quite damaged, but with only six stitches needed, she should be ok. Amazingly, x-rays showed no broken bones. Her injuries, however, did include a concussion, multiple lacerations, headache, and whip lash causing neck and back pain. Our

Kim was alive and would recover. That was by far our most important news. We could breathe again.

Truly, this was an amazing report considering she had been thrown off the bike at a speed of forty-five miles per hour. We later heard that death from motor bike accidents was the number one cause of death in Cozumel, a statistic that made us shudder.

Then, more good news followed. John had talked to the American Consulate, Homeland Security, and the State Department and reported they would be able to fly out the next day. This would actually place them back in Florida before our ship arrived in Miami. Our spirits lifted measurably with all this good news.

John met us at the port the morning after Christmas and drove us to a motel to see Kim who, having been released from the hospital, was resting. He warned us that she looked pretty bad. Both eyes were black and blue, lips and cheeks swollen, along with multiple lacerations and bruises. We were so happy to be reunited, to see her trying to press her puffy face into a smile. I joked with her that she would never have to wonder how her lips would look with a Botox treatment. They couldn't have been more swollen.

All through this crisis we saw the hand of God. Going as fast as she was on the motor bike, she should have been dead or severely injured with broken bones. It's a miracle she wasn't. In talking to her at home later, however, there was still something she was baffled by.

"Mom, I'm perplexed about something that I don't understand about my accident. I cannot figure out how I landed on the road and not in the ravine alongside the road. There was a steep drop off on the side of the road filled with craggy, pointed rocks. As I flew off the bike, I remember the trajectory in which I was being thrown. I was heading straight toward the cliff. In that split second, I knew if I went over, I would have been impaled by the rocks. Here's what puzzles me. How did I land facing the other way, face down on the road?" This had been her last thought before losing consciousness. She was sure she was heading over the cliff.

When Kim shared her confusion, chills ran up my spine. I immediately knew why she had been spared. It was later confirmed by her mother-in-law.

"Kim," I said through tears, "I think I know why you were on the road. For the past week, I have been memorizing Psalm 91:11-12. All week I felt almost driven by God to repeat it over and over. I remember wondering why this verse was being so impressed on my heart. Now, I believe God put it there as a prayer. Listen to what it says. *"For He will give His angels charge concerning you, to guard you in all your ways. They will bear you up in their hands, that you do not strike your foot against a stone."*

When I read that to Kim, it was an emotional moment for both of us as we realized it was God who had motivated me to repeatedly recite that very verse in preparation for what was to come. We felt now that the verse was prophetic. God had surrounded Kim with angels who guarded her from striking against the stones. It was His angels who had securely carried her to safety in their hands. God had sent angels to protect her from being thrown into the stony ravine. It was they who placed her safely onto the road and spared her life. Interestingly, John's mother also had a vision of angels coming to her aid and surrounding her which she later shared with Kim.

God's provision didn't stop there. For them to get back into the U.S. so easily was a miracle since they had no passports. As for my concerns about the standard of medical treatment in Mexico, a Florida doctor affirmed that the stitches looked good. Amazingly, Cozumel had just built a new hospital which partnered with an American hospital. Kim's care was quite adequate. It took her some time to recuperate fully, but I will never forget this eventful Christmas cruise, God's clear message of help from the Psalms, and the angelic provision God sent.

I've heard that trials don't build character. They reveal it. Truly, the character of my grandchildren was revealed that week. No one panicked. Everyone was patient and kind. They bonded together and looked for ways to serve one another. Everyone pitched in to help. It was such a blessing to watch them care for each other. Truly, the love of Christ was flowing through our whole family.

Writing a Book

I have to say I'm thankful that every trial in life does not involve a tragic situation. Some trials merely require waiting. Many times in Scripture, we are told to wait, to wait patiently, to wait for the Lord. When my mother started her journey with Alzheimer's, I had a strong inclination that I needed to journal her demise. It did not enter my mind at that time that it would later turn into a book, "Mother Has Alzheimer's." I just had a "knowing" that God wanted me to write down everything that happened. He even revealed to me that He planned for this to be a sort of "adventure in God," in that I could expect to see His hand at every turn. Indeed, that is exactly what happened.

The writing came easily, and I felt at the time that it was actually therapeutic. Watching a loved one fall prey to the devastation of Alzheimer's is both tragic and heartbreaking. The person I once knew as my mother became lost as the illness ravaged her mind. Writing helped me endure that season of life.

After my mother passed away, I began to think that my experience might be helpful to others who faced a similar type of journey. So, I typed up all my stories and the lessons I had learned and had them bound into a manuscript. Then, as God made me aware of people who might find comfort by reading it, I lent it out. Always, it was returned with kind comments. One friend wrote, "Betsy, I cannot thank you enough for sharing this book with me. Your ability to share your experience with your mother inspired and encouraged me. Thank you for touching my heart." Another friend encouraged me with these words, "God used your experience and words of wisdom to get me through some hard times…."

I began to acknowledge that God was clearly in the process of my writing. His voice was subtle and gentle, but I knew it was He who had allowed me to go through this experience with my mother and who nudged me to put it into a manuscript.

It was then that I began to consider having the book published. One by one, I mailed the manuscript to various publishers. Soon a cascade of rejection letters filled my mailbox. I became downcast. How could it be so clear that God led me to write, but now no one wanted to publish my book? It was then that I began praying in earnest. *God, I thought I heard from you to write this book. Why is everyone in the publishing business rejecting it?*

Almost immediately a new thought formed in my mind. *I asked you to write the book, Betsy. I didn't ask you to publish it at this time.*

Wow…that took me off guard. God didn't want me to publish the book? I had no rational idea why, but decided, ok, I'll stop sending it out then. Time went on. Years passed by. Twenty years to be exact. Then, one morning I was reading a Christian magazine and noticed an ad for self-publishing. Something welled up in my heart, and I sensed that now was the time. Perhaps the waiting period was over.

I asked Bill for his support, and he immediately said, "Yes, I've always felt you should publish your book. I think it would be helpful to a lot of people. Why don't you research several self-publishing houses and compare what they offer."

"Would you be willing to help me edit it?" I asked.

"I would be happy to," he gladly responded without hesitation.

With that, I began to pray and research. Quickly, I found a self-publisher that looked promising and gave them a call. Within days, I was on my way. It was a lot of work, a lot of hours rewriting, editing, and rewriting. Kim, also helped with editing, as did a friend, Sue. Twenty-one years after my mother passed away, my book was finally available to the public.

I look back at how it all started with a simple nudge from God. The Bible says in Psalm 20:4, *"May He grant you your heart's desire and fulfill all your counsel!"* I believe God enjoys giving us the desire of our heart. The way I think it works is this. First, He puts His desire in our heart, then He fulfills it. It's a win/win situation.

Summary

As you can see from my stories in this section…Camping in the Rain, Highway Trouble, Baby Saves Mother's Life, Ketchup Mess, Kim's Accident, and Writing a Book… in each circumstance, God spoke personal words to accomplish His purpose. In each story, God had a plan and revealed attitudes, direction, knowledge, and comfort, all depicting aspects of what a personal relationship with the Lord looks like, all done for His glory.

In our next chapter, let's turn a corner and see how God speaks through people.

Study Guide 5

1. Often, our first response to difficult circumstances is what?

2. What does the Bible say about hard circumstances in I Peter 4:12-13?

3. Where do we find victory and power? Philippians 3:10-11

4. A. What attitude is God looking for as we endure difficult situations according to I Thessalonians 5:16-18?

    B. Exactly how can this attitude be helpful?

5. A. How does James 1:2-3 say we should approach trials?

    B. What are we to gain from such an approach?

6. How would you relate the idea of a "sea of glass in the midst of fire" in Revelations 15:2 to a difficult trial?

7. Share a time God has spoken to you through circumstances?

CHAPTER 6

God Speaks Through People

"...Behold, He speaks forth with His voice, a mighty voice" (Ps. 68:33).

Cross Pollination

W E NEED PEOPLE. It's as simple as that. My friend, Cindy, explains this need in a unique way. She had acquired two pumpkin plants, but sadly, one of them died. While the other one lived and had leaves, it bore no fruit. Not understanding, I asked her why. She explained that without the other plant, there would be no cross pollination, and without cross pollination, there would be no fruit. Cindy is a person who sees spiritual lessons in many of life's experiences, so I knew further explanation was forthcoming.

"It's the same with relationships," Cindy explained. "Just as two pumpkins need each other to bear fruit, so we, as believers, also need one another."

One of the beautiful aspects of my relationship with Cindy is that we have been cross pollinating for years. God will show her something, and she will bless me with what He said. Then, He will speak into my life, and I will share it with her. I love that about our friendship. I think that's the way God meant friendships to be...cross pollinating and thereby, bearing fruit.

By ourselves, we may look good just as the pumpkin plant was green and had leaves, but where was the fruit? People need people. Many times, God will speak to us through other people and use the message to pollinate our life. I imagine we can all think of times when this kind of transaction has taken place.

Three Ways God Speaks Through People

One of the most common ways the Lord speaks to us is through other people but exactly how does He do that? For the purposes of this book, let's look at three ways defined in I Corinthians 12:7, 8 and 10, *"But to each one is given the manifestation of the Spirit for the common good. For to one is given the **word of wisdom** through the Spirit, and to another the **word of knowledge** according to the same Spirit...and to another **prophecy**...."*

The spiritual gifts listed in I Corinthians 12 were given by the Holy Spirit for the purpose of building up the body. We need each other. The principle is really quite simple. We give and we receive. Each of us has strengths and gifts, but we each have needs as well. We need others and they need us. The gifts enable us to bring God's perspective into life's situations. One such time, when I very much needed a word of wisdom, was when my mother had Alzheimer's. A word of wisdom is helpful when we meet a situation we don't know how to handle, one where we need enlightenment, an impartation of God's understanding. Let me tell you about my "Angel in Disguise."

Angel in Disguise *(Story taken from my book, "Mother Has Alzheimer's")*

Long before my mother's diagnosis of Alzheimer's disease, I noticed some unusual symptoms: memory loss, disorientation, confusion, paranoia, misplacing items, and getting lost. After much discussion, my sister, Cynthia, and I made the difficult decision to move Mother into a retirement home. We agreed that I would make the trip to her home in Arizona to prepare her for the move. I had mixed feelings. I knew Mother could no longer safely live alone, yet I felt troubled at the thought of robbing some of her independence.

As I pondered my visit to help her move, I sought God for advice as to how to manage my mother in her failing state of mind. Sorting and packing her belongings for the move would be difficult work. With Mother's mind slipping, her aptitude for clarity in communication concerned me. Even in recent phone conversations, I felt unsure how to respond to her much of the time.

On the day I traveled to Arizona, I boarded the plane and settled into my seat, continuing to pray as I still had not received an answer. *Please God, show me the best and kindest way to handle my mother.* Little did I know that God had already handpicked a sweet elderly lady to sit next to me, a lady who would give me just the wisdom I would need.

As the plane took off, I began to talk to my seatmate, Martha. She must have been in her seventies. As she told me about recently losing her husband, I felt comfortable enough to share with her the reason for my trip.

"I'm headed to Phoenix," I began, "to help my mother arrange the sale of her house and to pack her things for a move. She's failing mentally. There will be so many of her things I will have to give away or throw away. My mother's mental state and ability to understand seem to have diminished, but I want to involve her as much as possible in the moving process. I am wondering if you have any advice for me in handling a mother whose mind is failing."

Almost immediately, I knew that God was in the conversation. Words of wisdom flowed from the lips of my new friend as she outlined five practical things I could do. As the plane landed in Phoenix, I felt I'd gained more wisdom during that flight than I could have hoped for. I recalled James 1:5 *"But if any of you lacks wisdom, let him ask of God, who gives to all generously and without reproach, and it will be given to him."* God had equipped me for the task ahead, and I wondered if my friend was really an "angel in disguise."

Each piece of her advice became significant during my week with Mother. Her words, sealed in my mind, had prepared me for each incident that arose. The five choice pieces of wisdom, listed below, proved to be a valuable source of strength during that demanding and strenuous week. Truly, God spoke to me through Martha's words.

1. "Preserve your mother's dignity and integrity at any cost," she began. Aware of this principle, I tried to involve Mother in as many decisions as possible. One afternoon, I assigned her the project of sorting through her jewelry and selecting pieces to be stored. Within minutes, I realized this was asking too much. She ended up playing with her jewelry for an hour. In the end, it was in a tangled pile on the carpet. She had a wonderful time, and though nothing was accomplished, she felt she had a part in the process. Her dignity was intact.

2. "Be sure to initiate affection, hugs, and hand holding," my new friend suggested. "Don't wait for her to initiate. In her mental state, she may not." Each morning I took Mother's hands in mine as we prayed for the day ahead. During the day, I often hugged her and patted her arm. Initiating touch kept us close throughout the week.

3. "Let love be your guide to maintaining peace and unity, and make a commitment not to argue," Martha wisely advised. These words kept our relationship balanced and sweet more than once during the week.

Late one hot afternoon, feeling exhausted from sorting, I reacted to a bizarre comment Mother made. "You must be confused!" I blurted.

"No, dear, you are the confused one," she snipped.

Immediately, I remembered my angel's words, "Don't argue; maintain peace and unity." With a deep breath, I regained composure, smiled at Mother and said, "How about we take a break and have a cup of tea."

4. "Remember, the last thing to go is hearing. Be careful what you say when she is near," my angel counseled. "It's so easy to talk about a person with Alzheimer's while in their presence. Yet, people with

Alzheimer's often have no problem hearing. When they hear hurtful things, they react on the inside just like a normal person."

Many times during the week, I shook my head at things Mother did or said, and the temptation was sometimes there to talk about her to a visiting friend. Due to Martha's advice, however, I tried to be careful what I said in Mother's presence. In her paranoid state, she often came into a room asking about our conversation. Convinced we were talking about her, she needed reassurance, so I tried to say only things she could hear.

5. "Reading the twenty-third Psalm can be soothing to an older person," Martha exhorted as her final word of wisdom. I found that reading Scripture was a great comfort to Mother that week. Because Bible verses are spiritually discerned, they seemed to transcend Mother's mental difficulties and minister directly to her spirit. When she was agitated, I read from the Psalms, and it seemed to settle her.

Because of the wise words God sent to me through my angel in disguise on the plane, my week took on a refreshing dimension. Aware of God's presence and His guidance made all the difference.

Reflection on Words of Wisdom

God imparted words of wisdom to me through Martha's gracious words on the plane. Her words, as Cindy would agree, cross pollinated with my heart, and indeed, bore much fruit that week. Martha's words were not only practical for my circumstance, but they sustained me during an otherwise very tedious week. Her reminders enabled me to remain calm and agreeable. Although they were not specific Bible verses, they lined up well with biblical principles. They also bore the fruit of love, unity, and peace in both my mother and myself. John 15:5 affirms the idea of fruit bearing when Jesus said , *"I am the vine, you are the branches; he who abides in Me, and I in him, he bears much fruit; for apart from Me you can do nothing."*

Without hearing God's specific words of wisdom for that particular situation, I could have had a frustrating, strife filled week. Instead, I was focused, helping Mother stay calm as well. Although the week was difficult in many ways, I look back on it as a week of victory. Hearing God's voice made the difference.

Friendship Dilemma

One of my all time favorite stories involved a time when God gave Bill a word of wisdom that ministered to our daughter, Laurie, in the midst of a difficult grade school situation. At the age of ten, Laurie, being new to Southern California, had befriended Michele, a girl in our neighborhood. It didn't take long for us to notice that this new friend had a rebellious streak against adult authority and supervision.

One late afternoon as I was preparing dinner, I received a phone call from Laurie. I had given her permission to walk with Michele to a local strip mall near our neighborhood. Now, it was nearing six o'clock, past the time she was to be home. Although glad to hear from her, I was concerned when she informed me that she and Michele wanted to stay and have dinner at the mall. She wasn't so much calling to ask as to tell me this was the plan.

Trying not to over-react that a ten-year-old would even consider this appropriate, I insisted she come right home. This was not the first time Michele had tried to sway Laurie into something she knew we would not agree to. One recent evening, we had been blindsided when we allowed Laurie to go to a local carnival with Michele. Since one of her parents was taking them, we assumed he would also accompany the girls and wait as they rode the various carnival rides. It was only when Laurie arrived home that we learned Michele's parent had just dropped them off at the carnival and later picked them up. Definitely not appropriate for ten-year-old children in Southern California.

Now, arriving home from the mall, Laurie recounted a conversation she and Michele had just engaged in. "Michele thinks you're too tight with me. She says you need to loosen up so that I can do whatever I want. She says she goes where she wants to and does whatever she wants." Since Laurie related this news with softness, without an attitude, I could see she was questioning the validity of Michele's advice. She was merely reporting the conversation to me.

As you can imagine, by now, I was seeing all kinds of red flags in this relationship. An independent child, Michele rarely heeded any attempt of parental authority. Living with her father, he, unfortunately, chose to hold the reigns loosely with his daughter. Although Laurie counted obedience as important, we could see this friend was influencing her thinking in a negative way. Going along with Michele's ideas sometimes got Laurie in trouble. Interestingly, she was also becoming increasingly frustrated with Michele's ability to manipulate her.

Concerned about this negative influence in Laurie's life, Bill and I prayed. The Lord soon spoke to Bill, and a plan of action unfolded. The word of wisdom he received was a simple plan that affected Laurie in a very sweet and beneficial way. We still reminisce about God's special work in this situation.

Over the years, Bill had made a habit of separately taking the girls on "dates" for dinner every couple of months. All dressed up, the girls in their best Sunday clothes and Bill in coat and tie, they headed off to a destination restaurant. These memorable times with Daddy were always looked forward to with anticipation. Bill, wisely, used this carved out time to cultivate his relationship with each of his daughters. Keeping watch over their souls held a high priority with him, so he always tried to plan and direct conversation to meaningful subjects.

On this particular date with Laurie, once they had settled into their booth and finished ordering their meals, she asked, "What are we going to talk about tonight, Daddy?"

Looking at the anticipation in her eyes, Bill smiled at her innocence and replied, "Let's talk about friendship tonight, Laurie. You've had some good friends over the years. Let's pick one and list some qualities that made the relationship special."

Pulling a pen from his pocket and a piece of note paper, Bill prepared to itemize her list. The evening was off to a good start.

Choosing Theresa, a next door neighbor and friend in the previous town we lived in, Laurie recounted some of her traits. "Theresa was loyal, Daddy. She helped me do the right things and that made me feel good about myself. She was kind, and I could trust her." As Laurie continued sharing Theresa's unselfish and honest qualities, Bill's plan unfolded.

"That's a great list, Laurie. Sounds like Theresa built you up and brought out the best in you," Bill surmised.

"Yes, Daddy, I think she did."

Handing the list to Laurie, Bill continued, "Laurie, I would like you to look over this list again, and tell me how you think your relationship with Michele stacks up against the character qualities you just listed."

As she took a few moments to scrutinize the list, reading again the qualities one by one, a light bulb went on in Laurie's heart. Slowly lifting her eyes, she commented with animation, "Oh, I don't think my relationship with Michele is anything like this, Daddy!"

Gently, Bill continued the conversation. Obviously, God was at work. It was going incredibly better than he had even hoped.

"Laurie, perhaps you need to do some thinking about your friendship with Michele. Maybe some decisions need to be made."

Through the word of wisdom God had given Bill on how to handle a potentially sticky issue, Laurie had seen the truth for herself and was now able to make her own decision about the relationship. Within the next weeks, we noticed visits with Michele occurred less often. Having observed the harmful fruit of this friendship, Laurie made the decision to allow it to taper off.

As I pondered how Bill had dealt with Laurie regarding her relationship with Michele, I was amazed at God's creativity. Left to our own understanding, we might have been tempted to give Laurie a directive to terminate the relationship immediately. In retrospect, I'm guessing that approach might have ended badly. Being told "no" to the relationship could have driven her to want it more.

God had a better plan that led Laurie to her own decision. Isn't it like God to "lead" us to right thinking and then right decisions? His ways are higher than our ways, and His thoughts are higher than ours.

The word of wisdom Bill received on how to approach this difficult issue enabled Laurie to think through her situation from a fresh perspective and draw her own conclusions. God spoke a word of wisdom to Bill and gave a gentle and tactful solution. When God speaks and we follow, He provides the power to accomplish His will. God was right in the center of Bill's conversation with Laurie that night with a helpful word of wisdom. He would say that having God direct his path made all the difference.

Word of Knowledge

A second way God can speak into our lives is through the word of knowledge (I Cor. 12:8). A word of knowledge is an awareness of information which no person has revealed. It is the ability to know something that we would have no way of knowing on our own. God sometimes reveals the knowledge necessary to understand a situation so that we can comfort, exhort, or build a person up. This gift is especially helpful for people in leadership, counseling, or mentoring roles. As with all the gifts, it must edify or encourage, never condemn.

When I teach a Bible class, there are times the Holy Spirit will give me something fresh to say that I had not planned as part of a lesson. I recognize that as a word from God specifically for the edification of the class. God is endlessly creative in how He uses others to speak into our lives. We need only to open our ears to hear and receive from Him.

Paul's Word about a Shipwreck

The biblical account of Paul's voyage at sea provides a classic example of a word of knowledge in operation. In Acts 27, we see Paul and his sailing companions tossed about by a violent wind.

Storm-tossed for several days, they began to pitch cargo overboard in an attempt to keep the boat afloat.

Hope for rescue waned until one night the Lord sent an angel to Paul with a word of knowledge. The angel said, *"...Do not be afraid, Paul; you must stand before Caesar; and behold, God has granted you all those who are sailing with you"* (Acts 27:24). In verse twenty-two, Paul reported to the men onboard that the ship would be damaged, but all the men would be safe. When Paul reiterated this word of knowledge to the sailors, it brought comfort and encouragement to the two hundred and seventy-six men on board.

In the midst of a trial, Paul received a word that made his ordeal bearable. He knew what was going to happen which enabled him to help the other men weather the storm. His rhema word brought reassurance to men who feared they would otherwise drown (Acts 27:22-44).

Pastor's Wife's Inner Turmoil

Not all trials are outward as in the ship wreck predicament. Sometimes, a word of knowledge can help with issues of the soul. Such was the case with Jane. I had never met Jane, but I knew she was the wife of a local pastor.

One morning, a mutual friend called to ask if I would come to her home to pray with her and Jane concerning Jane's emotional upheaval. Hopping in my car, I went right over, met Jane, and found her totally overwrought about life. After talking for fifteen or twenty minutes, I didn't have a clue concerning the "real" problem.

"Let's pray," I suggested, "and ask God for a word of knowledge as to what we're dealing with." We all bowed our heads and began earnestly seeking the Lord for knowledge and wisdom.

After several minutes, some words began to form in my mind - bitterness, anger, hatred, unwillingness to forgive, and depression. Looking up at Jane, I gently asked her if she felt any of those words applied to her situation.

"Yes," she admitted, bursting into tears. "They all do. I'm very angry and bitter, and I feel depressed."

We asked her if she wanted to deal with these negative attitudes. After further conversation, she confessed there was someone she had not forgiven. We all felt that was the root of her problem. She prayed, repented of her sin, and asked God to help her forgive.

How did we know how to minister to Jane? God gave us a word of knowledge. There are times when we have no idea how to help a person. It can be frustrating to want to bring life to a situation but to have no clue how to proceed. On our own, we couldn't discern what troubled Jane. Her situation sounded confusing, but God knew her heart. He chose to give us words of knowledge so we could lead her in prayer and help her begin to resolve what was clearly troubling her.

Priesthood of Believers

In I Peter 2:9, we learn that, as believers, we are called to be a kingdom of priests. Revelation 1:6 says, *"And He has made us to be a kingdom, priests to His God and Father..."* (See also 5:10). In the Old Testament, under the old covenant of law, only certain people could function in the role of a priest. But that all ended when Christ died. At that time the veil in the temple that separated the people from the Holy of Holies where God dwelled, was ripped in two, giving the people access to God. What a glorious thought, that we can freely and confidently enter God's presence anytime, anyplace. As believers, we have a permanent right of entry to the throne of grace. Hebrews 4:16 says, *"Therefore let us draw near with confidence to the throne of grace, so that we may receive mercy and find grace to help in time of need."* What a wonderful assurance of access to God.

One of the roles of a priest is the privilege of talking to God on behalf of people and talking to people on behalf of God. If we are willing to listen, God has many things to reveal to us. In the case of Jane, we were able to go confidently before God, seek His counsel, and deliver the insightes He showed us to a troubled woman.

High School Sunday School

When our daughters were in high school, I became burdened about their Christian education. Since they attended public school, Bill and I felt responsible for building biblical principles into their lives. However, as I questioned the girls on things I thought they should know, it distressed me to find they didn't know as much about the Bible as I had hoped.

Their Sunday school teacher enjoyed the teenagers, but unprepared with a lesson, he spent the class time each week just talking to them. The Bible, unfortunately, was rarely the focal point of their discussions.

I began to pray, asking God for direction. *How can I get your Word into the girls, Lord?* I labored in prayer seeking the Lord and His answer. I didn't have a clue what to do until one day, as I prayed, a still small voice whispered, *Why don't you teach the Sunday school class?*

Oh, no, Lord. I don't think that would be a good idea, was my immediate reply. *I don't relate well to teens.* The Lord, always a gentleman, didn't press me, but His words gently nudged my heart. Later, as I prayed, the thought came to mind, *sometimes you are the answer to your own prayer.*

In time, the idea of teaching the class began to seem like a possibility. If God was calling me, then surely He would give me the strength to do it. Soon, I approached our pastor and asked him what he thought about the idea. Delighted, he responded with enthusiasm. Aware that the present teacher chose not to teach from the Scriptures, the thought of me teaching the Bible to the teens sounded wonderful to him.

"There's just one problem," he confided, "The present teacher really enjoys the youth and is not planning to leave his position."

"Oh, I see," I puzzled. "Well, I guess if the Lord wants me to teach, He'll open the way."

We agreed to leave the situation with God, watching with interest to see what He would do. Within a few months, we were surprised to learn that, after many years with the teens, the teacher had decided to resign his Sunday school position. This left the class open for me to teach. Another lady in the church agreed to co-teach the book of Mark with me. It turned out to be a wonderful year of study as we used only the Bible as our teaching resource. Both of my daughters later expressed that this class had marked a turning point in their spiritual lives.

When God plants a thought in our heart, He has a definite plan He wants to fulfill. Growth, change and blessing follow His ways. The Lord gave me a specific word to teach the class. The word of direction came to me as a thought in my mind during a time of prayer and intercession on behalf of my children. It would seem that sometimes when we get an idea that "somebody in the church" or a pastor should do something, it may actually be a word for us to be involved. Yes, we may be the answer to our own prayer. If we are willing to listen, God will surely clarify.

A Prophetic Word from Mary

Sometimes a word of knowledge is similar to a prophetic word. An occasion that particularly ministered to me happened during a time when I felt restless about my life. Having spent several weeks praying, I discerned that the root of my confusion lay in an uncertainty about my life's direction. Was I moving in the direction God had for me? I felt confused as to whether I was in the center of God's will.

Bill and I planned to attend a house group meeting one night that week, so I appealed to the Lord to speak to me through someone there. I hadn't told anyone what was on my heart. I was hoping the Lord would speak to me through an unsolicited person.

The group spent the first part of the meeting singing and worshipping. Following our worship time, we prayerfully waited upon God. Mary, a lady in the group, whom I did not know well, began to speak a prophetic word. Unbeknownst to her, God used her words to bring me both comfort and peace as the *"God of all comfort"* spoke directly to my heart (I Cor. 1:3).

Here is what she said: "The Lord wants someone here to know that they should continue in the direction they are going in their life," she said. "I feel God is also saying to this person that if He has a different direction, He will reveal it, so they don't need to be concerned about missing His will."

Without knowing it, Mary brought me a word from the Lord, a word that spoke directly to my question. With that word, my disquieted heart began to rest. I moved back into a place of trusting Him to direct my path. I was at peace again. God promises to reveal, direct, and establish our way (Prov. 8:6, II Thess. 3:5, I Pet. 5:10). His words through Mary that night moved my heart out of confusion and disorder into peace and faith.

A description of prophesy is found in I Corinthians 14:3, *"But one who prophesies speaks to men for edification and exhortation and consolation."* Her prophetic word edified and built me up. It exhorted and encouraged me to trust God. Her words consoled and comforted me, reminding me that I was where God wanted me to be.

Mary didn't realize what her words meant to me until I phoned her the next week. She expressed how blessed she felt to hear that God had used her in someone's life. She had been praying that God would use her more in ministry to others. Sounds like cross-pollination to me.

Encouragement for Dave

As a young man, Dave heard God's voice as a call to become a pastor. He attended Bible school and ministered in churches for many years. Then, due to circumstances in his life, he left the ministry and took a secular job. It wasn't long, however, before he began to long to return to the role of pastor. Months rolled into years, yet to his disappointment, God chose not to provide the opportunity.

Feeling discouraged, Dave explored different avenues, hoping to find an open door, but all doors remained closed for full-time ministry. He desperately needed a word of encouragement from the Lord. Unbeknownst to him, he was about to receive one.

Attending a Hunter Healing Explosion event, Dave participated as a healing counselor. At one point, the Hunters called all pastors and their wives to come forward for a blessing. Dave's pastor encouraged him and his wife, Lynn, to go forward even though Dave was not currently a pastor in a church at the time. With that prompting, though, they made their way up to the front of the auditorium and received a pastoral blessing. However, it was later in the evening that the Lord chose to speak to Dave in a way that became a breakthrough.

When the evening drew to a close, Dave and Lynn started to walk out of the auditorium. As they moved toward the crowded exit, a couple they had never met stopped them. "You don't know us," they explained. "When you went forward for prayer as a pastor, God drew our attention to you and gave us a word for you." Curiosity captivated Dave's interest. Several hundred people had come up during that time of prayer. Why had God picked him out?

"God told me that you're a shepherd without a flock," the woman kindly spoke. "He wants you to know that this is just for a season and that He is preparing a people for you."

Awestruck, Dave left the meeting with renewed hope. These people couldn't have known he wasn't presently in a pastor's role in a church. They had never seen each other before, and after all, he had gone up front for prayer for pastors.

This word from the Lord greatly encouraged and comforted Dave. God met him at the point of his need. Dave now felt reassured in the Lord's long term plan for his life, even though he had yet to see it come about at that point.

The word of knowledge Dave had received gave him hope as he then waited with expectation through the dry season he experienced. Within a few years time, God did provide a pastorate position for him. He has continued in that church for a number of years, blessing, loving, and counseling many people. But he will never forget the kindness of a woman he didn't know who took the time to hear God's voice and bring a message of hope and encouragement to him.

Reflection

These examples of the word of knowledge, word of wisdom, and prophetic word comprise three avenues God uses to speak to people. It is interesting to note that I Corinthians 12:8 says "word" of wisdom and "word" of knowledge, not just gifts of wisdom and knowledge. I have heard people say that a person with these gifts simply knows a lot about the Bible. I would have to disagree. The gifts in I Corinthians 12 are all supernatural gifts that we can only receive from God. Anyone can read and gain knowledge of the Bible through personal study. "Word of knowledge" is different. It is a God given ability to hear His voice in a way that will benefit a person or situation.

We also know from scripture that knowledge, by itself, puffs up, causing a boastful heart. When God gives a word of knowledge, it is a humbling experience, not an occasion to brag about personal knowledge.

In the same way, a word of wisdom is not natural wisdom gained from living life. We know that the wisdom of this world is foolishness to God, so it is good to separate words that come from God from words that the world gives.

As you have read about ways God speaks to or through people, the Lord may be stirring your heart, bringing to mind times when you have been aware that you seemed to know something about someone or a situation that you clearly had not been informed about through any outside source. You may also recall a time when you just seemed to gain wisdom and knew how to solve a sticky problem. Or you may remember a time when you offered words of comfort, or exhortation to a friend. You somehow knew that only God could have revealed certain information to you. That is what hearing God's voice is all about.

Study Guide 6

1. A. From I Corinthians 12:7-8 and 14:3, name three ways God can speak through people.

   B. Explain each of these three terms.

   C. Share a time God has used one of these gifts to help in your life.

2. A. Look at Paul's experience in Acts 27. What word did the angel give him to deliver to the 276 men on board?

   B. As Paul related the word of knowledge to the men, how do you think it affected them?

3. God is interested in outward problems and inner problems. How could a word from God help an inner conflict?

4. God promises to reveal, direct, and establish our way. Write in your own words what each of these verses says to you.

   A. Prov. 8:6

   B. II Thess. 3:5

   C. I Pet. 5:10

5. Has there been a time when you have spoken into someone's life? Please share it.

CHAPTER 7

God Speaks Through Visions and Dreams

> *"...Your young men shall see visions, and your old men shall dream dreams" (Acts 2:17).*

Visions and Dreams in the Bible

SINCE THIS SUBJECT is not one that is often spoken of in most churches, we need to first establish that it is biblical. Were dreams and visions experienced by people living in biblical times? Yes! They played an important role in the unfolding of many biblical events. They repeatedly served as a tool through which God revealed important information and direction.

Visions and dreams in the Bible were one of God's foremost means of speaking through the prophets. Numbers 12:6 gives this account, *"...Hear now My words. If there is a prophet among you, I, the Lord, shall make Myself known to him in a vision. I shall speak with him in a dream."*

We know that Joseph received a dream early in his life where God revealed that his brothers would one day bow down to him (Gen. 37:5-10). This dream sustained Joseph through many hardships. He knew God had disclosed His plan, and he trusted Him to be faithful.

Later, the Pharaoh of Egypt had two very puzzling dreams which Joseph was able to interpret (Gen. 41). They concerned lean and fat cattle and plump and thin ears of grain. Through his dreams, God warned of a famine that was to come. This knowledge enabled Egypt to prepare. God chose not only to give a message but also a blueprint of action that would ultimately save the Egyptians and the Israelites.

God gave Daniel knowledge of future events through visions and dreams. Puzzled by a dream he had, King Nebuchadnezzar called on Daniel to interpret. First, Daniel gave God the credit for being the One who reveals mysteries, then he interpreted Nebuchadnezzar's dream as one of coming events. In fact, many prophecies, revealed through those visions and dreams, are still future to us. They deal with end times, the second coming of Christ and the throne of God.

In the transfiguration of Jesus, the three attending disciples, Peter, James, and John saw a vision. Elijah and Moses appeared talking with Jesus. In Matthew 17:9, Jesus referred to the event as a vision when He said, *"...tell the vision to no one until the Son of Man has risen from the dead."* God used this vision to impact the disciples with the awesome glory and singularity of Jesus.

Paul received a vision when God caught him up into the third heaven. He heard unspeakable information concerning future events (II Cor. 12). Paul was so struck by what he saw that he came away with a new perspective on strength and weakness and determined to allow Christ to shine through him regardless of circumstances.

Peter received a vision, recorded in Acts chapter ten where God told him to eat animals that He had formerly considered unholy. Through the vision, God revealed that Peter was to receive Gentiles, whom he had long regarded as unclean. God used this vision to change an attitude in Peter that was deeply ingrained in his thinking. Peter gained a greater understanding of God's plan, and his change of heart enabled him to authenticate and endorse Paul's ministry to the Gentiles.

Visions and dreams in Scripture were often used for astounding purposes, but what about today? Before Christ and the coming of the Holy Spirit, God spoke through certain chosen people, sometimes using visions and dreams. This is well explained in Hebrews 1:1, 2, *"God, after He spoke long ago to the fathers in the prophets in many portions and in many ways, in these last days has spoken to us in His Son...."* From these verses, we glean that God's most significant way to speak to us today is through His Son, Jesus.

But still, is there biblical authority to expect visions and dreams in our modern day church experience? I suppose that depends. Do you think we are in the latter days before Christ's return? If your answer is, "Yes," then there is biblical precedent for dreams and visions today. Acts 2:17 speaks to this issue: *"'And it shall be in the last days,' God says, 'that I will pour forth of my spirit on all mankind, and your sons and your daughters shall prophesy, and your young men shall see visions, and your old men shall dream dreams.'"*

It is interesting to note that this verse in Acts 2 is confirmation of Joel 2:28 in the Old Testament. It reveals that God has a desire to continue in the church what He spoke through the prophets long before the idea of the church was even known.

To me, one of the most exciting present day accounts of dreams involves people in Muslim countries. Muslims are very open to the idea of dreams and visions because their founder, Mohammad, formed the religion of Islam as the result of a dream. I have read several articles about how Jesus is visiting Muslims in their dreams.

Interestingly, this has become a wonderful tool for Christian evangelists and missionaries to engage in conversation with Muslims. In some eastern countries, dreams of Jesus are so common that missionaries have become bold in approaching Muslims by asking, "Have you had a dream?" Often the reply is "Yes," which gives the missionary a comfortable way to transition by asking to hear about the dream. Usually, the Muslim is eager to share and does not understand what his dream means. This, of course, provides a platform for missionaries to share the gospel. It is a beautiful approach to ministry with people who otherwise might be closed to hearing the good news of salvation. If you would like to read an article on this subject, one I recommend is from Charisma Magazine, December

2012. It's entitled, "Why Revival is Exploding Among Muslims," and can be found online.

A word of caution may be in order here. I don't believe God ever intended for us to seek after visions and dreams. These just come to people, usually unexpectedly, without warning. The Bible tells us to seek after the Lord, not an experience. Then, if He chooses to bless us with a vision or dream, it is His choice. We should be open to receive from Him, but should be careful to let Him take the initiative.

How can I know if a dream or vision is from God? Scripture exhorts us to test the spirits. This means that if we or someone we know has had a vision or dream, it should be tested to be sure it is from God. I John 4:1 puts it this way, *"Beloved, do not believe every spirit, but test the spirits to see whether they are from God; because many false prophets have gone out into the world."*

Anything in Christianity, including dreams and visions, can be tested by the response to two questions. We must first ask: Did it bring glory to God, or did it draw attention to self, another person, or an organization? The second question is: What kind of fruit did it produce? If the dream or vision involves something in the future, fruit may not be revealed until later. If the end result glorifies God and brings about fruit that lines up with the character of God and the truth of the Bible, we can trust by faith that God sent it.

Trip to Europe

One summer, Bill approached me with a plan. "Vic and Ruth Ann (our pastor and wife) are planning to go to Europe in the fall to visit Christians in some of the Eastern Bloc, former communist countries. They would like us to go along. What do you think?"

I gulped and replied, "I'll have to pray about it."

The more I thought about this trip, the more I didn't want to go. Frankly, I had no desire to leave my comfortable home and travel to unknown lands.

Besides lack of interest, there were other hold backs as well. Who would take care of our eight year old son? And what if I couldn't catch up on my sleep? The last overseas trip I'd taken was miserable. With the demanding schedule, I always felt tired.

I also convinced myself that, unable to speak the languages, I would likely experience constant stress and continual boredom. Envisioning hours of difficult communication all but traumatized me and certainly didn't give me a good feeling about going on this trip. Though I prayed and prayed, I could not shake my fear and concerns. Not wanting to drag down the group with my negative attitudes, I felt they would all be better off if I just stayed home. I would certainly be more comfortable and happier too. Meanwhile, everyone I talked to said I should go.

"It will be such a stretching and expanding opportunity for you, Betsy," they would say. "Your eyes will be opened to so many new experiences. Just think how it will help you in your ministry."

"I just don't see it," I would reply. "I see no reason to go."

My vision was clearly blocked by my fears, which to me were all reasonable. Reasonable, in retrospect, if you don't count faith and the reality that the Lord would be going on the trip with me.

Time passed and I needed to make a decision. One morning, I decided to seek God's will through fasting and praying. No sooner had I sat down to pray than that still small voice began to fill my thoughts.

Betsy, I want you to go on this trip by faith. Your trust has been in your feelings. You will not have the feelings you are seeking before you go. I want you to trust Me and go by faith, believing that I have a plan.

As I pondered the Lord's direction, I also weighed the fact that the two authorities in my life, my pastor and my husband, wanted me to go. While no one was insisting I go, I did want to honor and trust their influence in my life. After more prayer, I decided that I would choose to go by faith and not cave in to my feelings. At the time, that was a big step for me to take.

I think of Joshua crossing the Jordan River. In Joshua 1:1-3, he was told by God that, *"Every place on which the sole of your foot treads, I have given it to you...."* I felt I was being given a similar test of faith, certainly not as grandiose, but still a test of faith. Joshua didn't just put his toe in the water. He had to put in the full weight of his foot. My water consisted of my own trepidation.

Announcing my affirmative decision to Bill, I knew I had heard from God. However, although I said, "Yes," my feelings about the trip remained the same. Right up to the day we left, people would ask, "Aren't you excited about this trip?" To their disappointment, my consistent reply was, "No, not really". However, I had made a commitment to myself that no matter what happened on this journey, I would maintain a positive attitude for the sake of the others. That was the least I could do…suffer silently. Well, maybe I hadn't put my whole foot in the water just yet.

As for my excuses, I noticed the Lord began to provide answers even before we left. Friends agreed to watch Mike for the two weeks we would be gone. Ticket prices were agreeable, and arrangements were made with the people we would lodge with on our first stop in Frankfurt, Germany. As the trip began, God continued to provide answers for all my concerns.

We arrived in Germany early in the day and were provided with comfortable beds to catch a quick nap. By the second day, I felt refreshed and ready to participate in activities. To my amazement, everywhere we went in Germany, people spoke English. In meetings, an interpreter was always provided, so my anxiety about boredom was promptly alleviated.

Even though I had apprehension and had resisted for so many weeks, this trip turned out to be a trip of a lifetime. We stayed in the homes of people who had risked their lives for Jesus by smuggling Bibles across the border into communist, Eastern Germany. We stood at the Berlin Wall within months of its fall. We talked at length with a man imprisoned for his faith, now free and writing a book. We visited a former underground church in Prague and had the joy of singing the same praise choruses as we sing in America, they in their language, and we in English. Truly, the Holy Spirit was introducing a wave of worship around the world at that time.

God even provided several ministry opportunities for us. One lady we stayed with told us she felt God had sent us to visit her personally. We sat at tables and ate with believers from several countries. We all exalted and bowed to the same God.

Another lady told us how her husband had been taking Bibles into the Eastern Bloc for many years. She only worried if he wasn't back by midnight each trip. He had been jailed at times but always continued his work. Another person told us the past seventeen years under communism had been very hard, but they had seen God at every turn. Always, their faith was strong. They trusted in God alone to meet their needs, and He had not disappointed them. Her concern, now that freedom was coming, was that the people of her country would be tempted to trust in worldly things and that false religions would rapidly overtake the people.

I was so touched by the faith of these sweet, committed believers. I began to realize I would never have had the privilege of meeting any of them if I had stayed home. I also would have missed out on many adventures God had prepared for us.

At one point in the trip, we were traveling along the Autobahn from Berlin to Frankfort, when Ruth Ann saw a sign for Erfurt. "Vic, we must stop here," she said. "We know a family who lives here. Remember, we met them at a camp in Switzerland some years ago." Vic exited the highway in Erfurt, a town with a population around a quarter of a million people. He had no clue where his friends lived as he had never been to Erfurt before. He only had an address.

Without the aid of a GPS, Vic decided to pray and ask God to direct us to the home of their friends. After praying, he said, "I need to turn right here." He made several more turns as he felt prompted. With one last turn, he saw a man whom he felt led to ask for directions. After a short conversation, the man pointed to a building on the opposite corner. It was the address we were looking for. We were all astounded. Vic had arrived at the exact location in a town of a quarter of a million people, in a town he had never been to before, all by faith and listening to God's directions for each turn.

We had no doubt it was God who had led us to the correct apartment. What a wonderful family we were privileged to meet there.

As soon as we entered the apartment, the wife picked up her broom and began to clunk the end of the handle on the ceiling. Within minutes, we heard a stampede of feet as people from the apartment above joined our gathering. What a party it was as they spontaneously, on the spur of the moment, served us food, gathered musical instruments, and insisted we all sing and praise God. It was a beautiful way to spend an afternoon, a highlight where God wanted to bless us with an unexpected turn on our journey.

On another occasion, Bill, Ruth Ann, Vic and I were having a Bible study. As we discussed some verses, Bill stated, "Some people see and then believe and others believe and then see."

Something instantly triggered in me, and I saw a vision of myself in a room. It was a comfortable room, and I felt happy there. However, beyond the room were several doors beckoning me to approach and walk through. No one was forcing me to walk toward any of the doors. I sensed I could stay in my comfortable room all my life, but of course, I would never know what lay beyond those doors without walking through them.

Immediately, I recognized God was speaking to me through the vision. The room represented my life. I could be comfortable, happy, and content in my little world with my familiar surroundings the rest of my life. That was one choice. Yet God had provided doors for me to walk through, doors that must be approached by faith. No knowledge of what lay beyond the doors would be granted without that step of faith, but each one seemed to promise an exciting adventure.

I realized that having walked through the door called, "Trip to Europe," I had seen the wonderful blessings the Lord provided. What if I had not gone on this trip? I never would have known what I missed. God wants His children to walk by faith, not by sight. What I anticipated "by sight," was an imagination that never happened. God provided for our son. I was caught up on my sleep, and the language wasn't a problem. I was neither bored nor stressed. As I had walked by faith, the Lord had enriched my life far beyond my expectations.

Since that time, God has opened up other amazing doors of opportunity. I wonder if I had resisted the first door, would I have continued to resist other doors due to fear and anxiety? I am so glad I walked through the first door... by faith.

God speaks through visions today. We need only listen. Through a simple picture in my mind, I was clearly reminded of God's desire for me to live by faith. God imprinted the truth of that vision on my heart. I learned that trust in God goes beyond feelings to faith that is willing to apply action.

What's the Difference?

During our trip to Europe, God spoke to me through a vision. Other times He chooses to speak to people through dreams. You might be wondering, what is the difference between a vision and a dream? Both are ways that God can communicate, but how do they differ from each other?

Visions are pictures received from God while we are awake. They involve a vivid mental image, either a still picture or a scene with action. We see or perceive something that probably isn't seen by others. Visions can carry a message from God that reveals a truth which we need to consider.

Dreams, on the other hand, are meaningful pictures experienced while asleep. Like visions, they may involve a word of knowledge or wisdom, revealed truth, revelation, or prophesy. They also line up with the written word and find their fulfillment in reality at a given time whether soon or far into the future.

While not every vision or dream is necessarily from God, they both have purpose in the kingdom of God. They impact the recipient in some way. Perhaps, they build faith and lead to a closer walk with God. Sometimes, God uses them to impart wisdom or knowledge in a situation. Other times, they provide encouragement or comfort. Perhaps, they might even point out an attitude that needs to be changed or they could challenge a pattern of thinking.

If a vision or dream is received for someone else, it should be shared in front of one or two witnesses. This dispels any unhealthy secretiveness or fear that may arise if it is not from God. If it is from God, it should also bear witness to the recipient. They should sense that the message represents something in their life that should be taken seriously. Remember, God always has purpose in the things He reveals to us.

The Baby

Greg, a young man with spiritual discernment and wisdom beyond his years, had an interesting dream a year or so after he and his wife, Lucy, had married. During a short term mission trip to the Dominican Republic, he dreamed one night that Lucy climbed on the scale and discovered she was eight or nine pounds overweight. In the dream, she went to the doctor to find out why. The doctor examined her and announced that she was pregnant.

When Greg had this dream, he and Lucy had no plans to have a baby anytime soon. Their lives were full, and their goals for the next number of years included many international ministry trips to get a feel for Christianity around the world. Since God had planted a desire for missions and foreign travel in them, having a family right away did not seem prudent. They were not thinking about children at all and had many reasons to put off having a child.

Greg decided to share the dream with Lucy, at which time she agreed that the timing for children was premature. Then Lucy received two visions, and in each of them she pictured a black haired baby boy cuddled on her lap.

God slowly began to change their hearts as they pondered the dream and the two visions. Though Greg resisted the idea at first, he admitted that his dream bore witness in his spirit. He felt it was from God.

The final proof of God's prodding came when a pastor in the Dominican Republic, whom Greg had never met, prophesied over him at a prayer meeting. "Don't be afraid," the man said. "God wants to give you a child."

God confirmed His plan for Greg through the words of a pastor who didn't know that God had already been dealing with them concerning a child. Greg left the meeting with excitement, expectation, and joy. He knew that God had confirmed to him through the dream, Lucy's visions, and finally the pastor's prophesy that a child was imminent in His plans for them. Greg and Lucy had their black haired, baby boy within the next year and what joy he has brought to their lives.

The Rope

Our daughter, Kim, had a vision of a thick rope being pulled apart. As the rope began to fray from the tension placed on it, she pictured each unraveled section being carefully tied back together, one by one. Soon the rope was stronger than ever with many new knots in place.

Concerned about the vision, Kim told her husband, John, about it. They both felt the Lord was preparing them for some future trials, the rope representing their marriage. They decided to spend time praying that God would see them through whatever He allowed in their lives. Soon, several difficult circumstances did arrive, but because of the vision, they felt prepared to face them. The hard times did tug at them and caused pressure (the frayed rope), but due to prayer, they were firmly bonded together and weathered the storm in victory.

Visions and dreams carry the potential to have a very powerful and meaningful impact on our lives. They can be welcomed because they are one of God's ways of imparting something to us. Often, they appear as a sort of picture, vivid and clear. With the vision or dream, God also gives interpretation. It may not come right away, but God eventually brings discernment and understanding.

This Can't Be My Thumb

Dennis, and his wife, Cami, are good friends we made through our church in Northern California. While attending a church reunion several years ago, Dennis related an incredibly interesting and unusual story about a vision he had experienced that almost defies belief. I'll retell it as a story with dialogue so you can experience the full impact of what happened.

"I can't get the bleeding to stop! This can't be happening. Why won't the bleeding stop?" Dennis plunged his hand into the bucket of cold water over and over. The crimson liquid was an instant reminder that the bleeding persisted.

Denial and shock were taking over his mind. "I need a tourniquet," he frantically mumbled to himself. Strapping his three inch, strong, leather railroad belt tight around his upper arm, he convinced himself this would solve the problem and the nightmare would be over. But the bleeding continued.

His neighbor, a fireman, burst into the house. "Dennis, what is going on, man? Oh, no…what have you done to your thumb?" he nearly shrieked, observing the pulsating flow of blood streaming into the pool of water. "I'm taking you to the hospital immediately."

"No, I'll be alright," came Dennis' lame, but clearly frightened reply.

"Absolutely not. Get in the car now. You're going to bleed to death."

Dennis loved chopping wood for the five wood burning fireplaces in the Bed and Breakfast he and his wife, Cami, owned. On chopping days, he could be found whacking away four or five hours at a time. It was kind of a therapeutic thing. This particular day he was holding a log in place when the wood moved slightly as the maul came crashing down for the split. It missed the wood, crushing and slicing his thumb in two, lengthwise.

Rushing into the emergency room, a doctor was immediately at attention, assessing the damage. "Well, Dennis, you have a couple of options. One, we can just amputate your thumb. Two, we can amputate your thumb and replace it with one of your big toes. Which will it be?" he asked in a matter of fact tone.

"I opt for none of those options," Dennis replied in a matter of fact tone. Another doctor came in and together they told him that an operation to reconnect his thumb would have less than a ten percent chance of success.

Regardless, Dennis was adamant in his prompt reply, "I choose reconnecting the thumb."

The doctors just shook their heads. "Alright, but you will be back here in several days begging us to amputate, because your thumb will be black by then."

The surgery to reconnect Dennis' thumb was tenuous, at best. There was no fingernail and no nerves or muscle were intact. Only about twenty percent of the skin on his thumb remained which could be sown together. Not much to work with. Dennis described his thumb as like a tube of toothpaste being run over with a steam roller. It was a precarious operation to be sure.

Upon finishing the five hour surgery, the doctor carefully wrapped the thumb and placed a metal cage over it for protection. Next, he wrapped the thumb to Dennis' hand and finally wrapped his hand against his abdomen for safe keeping. Dennis was sent home to heal. The prognosis didn't look good.

That night, though fitful, he eventually drifted off to sleep. With darkness at its deepest, Dennis was groggily stirred to wakefulness. *What in the world is that?* Rubbing the sleep from his eyes for clearer focus, *Are my eyes playing tricks on me? What is that bright light at the foot of my bed? What...?. Where did it come from? Wait...there seems to be a definite Presence about it... I....*

"Take the bandage off, Dennis," came a soft, audible voice which seemed to carry a measure of authority as it emanated from the light.

A mixture of quiet alarm and curiosity spun around in Dennis's mind. Yet, there was something comforting about this Presence, a familiarity, a knowing. Slowly, his heart softened as the identity of the Presence was revealed to his heart.

Gently, again, "Take off the bandage, Dennis."

"No, I don't want to," Dennis finally croaked, feeling edgy and unsure. "I don't want to see my thumb."

Soothingly, but with an air of powerful confidence, "Take off the bandage, my child."

Squeamishly, Dennis untied the wrapping around his abdomen. Once loosened, he began the slow, tedious job of removing the binding from his hand. With a shudder, he removed the metal cage.

Ok, I can do this, just one more layer. But what awaits me? No, I really don't want to see my crushed, distorted thumb! What is this all about? I feel like I'm having an out of body experience. Am I really awake? Ok, here goes.

Gingerly, the final layer of cloth dressing was unraveled. The light shed from the Presence would be enough to observe the damages.

What? Wait...this is impossible! I must be dreaming.

Heart pounding, Dennis raised himself up for a closer look. *I can't believe this. This defies logic. This kind of thing doesn't happen... but it has happened. My thumb is perfect. Now I know I must be dreaming. There are no stitches, no scars, no sign of an operation, no hint of an injury at all.* Turning his thumb to all sides... *How can this be? I can't believe my eyes. Praise God!*

Shaking, he couldn't take his eyes off his perfect thumb. Awaking Cami, they both sat amazed at what God had just done. Aloud, Dennis proclaimed, "I have just experienced a miracle. God, You are amazing! You are worthy of all praise, all honor, and glory. I worship you, my Lord. You have done the impossible."

The next morning, Dennis couldn't wait to head back to the doctor, metal cage in hand. Seeing him approach, the doctor assumed he had come in for the amputation, but then he noticed the happy smile on Dennis' face. He seemed joyful about something. That seemed odd.

"Just thought I'd drop by and return the cage," Dennis chuckled. "I won't need it, after all" he quipped as he held up his thumb for the doctor's inspection.

Aghast, the doctor nearly fainted. Looking at every side of Dennis' thumb, with awe he exclaimed, "This is truly a miracle."

"Yes, with man it's impossible, but with God all things are possible."

I assure you, this is a true story. I have seen his thumb. It is perfect. God does not have a problem with visions and dreams. He uses them at His will. They are part of how He chooses to, at times, communicate with people. While they are not to be sought for, neither are they to be ignored. We need to let God be God.

Angel of Comfort

While there are many reasons God uses visions, one of the most touching has to be to comfort those who mourn. On Christmas Eve, 2012, Jeannie, a dear friend of mine, lost her beloved husband, Jim, to the ravages of lung cancer. It was a hard fought battle, but after a few short months, Jim passed peacefully into the arms of our Lord.

Jeannie was concerned that Jim's passing would be especially hard on her special needs brother, Stevie. He and Jim had spent hours together a couple times a week for many years. On Sundays, they were often found working together on projects in Jim's workshop, doing yard work, or going on outings such as car shows. On Friday nights, they sometimes took in a movie, and, of course, shared a box of popcorn. As they enjoyed their common interests, a sweet bond had forged between them.

In the two months leading up to Jim's death, Stevie prayed faithfully each night for Jim's healing. With his simple faith, He believed God would answer, and Jim would soon be home. When the family realized that Jim's health was deteriorating rapidly, they began to pray not only for Jim but also that the Lord would somehow minister to Stevie to prepare him for what lay ahead.

On Christmas morning, Jeannie called Stevie's group home, one that Jim had provided for him years before, and told the staff the sad news about Jim's passing the night before, on Christmas Eve. Jeannie requested that she be the one to share the news with her brother. Stevie's house parent then related that, interestingly, Stevie had been up since sunrise and seemed very excited as he spoke of Jim being healthy and happy.

Jeannie's first thought was that Stevie believed God had answered his prayers, and he was looking forward to seeing Jim home from the hospital, ready to celebrate Christmas with the family. Jeannie's heart sank as she anticipated how hard it was going to be to tell Stevie about Jim's death when he must be thinking Jim would be joining them for the Christmas celebration.

Later in the day, as Stevie came in the front door of Jeannie's home, he was glowing, smiling, and excited. Dread again washed over Jeannie at the thought of breaking the news to him. Carefully, she explained that Jim had passed away the night before and that he was celebrating his first Christmas in heaven with Jesus.

To her surprise, Stevie continued to be excited and exclaimed "I know!"

Taken aback by this statement, Jeannie questioned, "How do you know that, Stevie?"

"An angel came to me last night and told me," he eagerly explained.

At first, Jeannie wondered if Stevie had dreamed about an angel, so she asked him to tell her more about it.

"Well," said Stevie, "first, my room filled with light, and it woke me up. Surprised, I sat up in my bed and put on my glasses to see what was happening. Right then, a man angel with wings, long flowing brown hair, and a deep, soft voice said, 'My brother Stevie, don't be afraid. I've come to tell you that Jim is in heaven. He is healthy and happy and does not want you to be sad.'"

Intrigued, Jeannie questioned further, "Did you stay in bed or get up?"

"I stood up so I could see him better. The angel was so large he filled the room from floor to ceiling," Stevie spoke with animation.

Over the months following Jim's death, instead of being lost in grief, Stevie was a continual encouragement to the family. His angelic experience had changed him. He was more at peace, and his bright countenance brought comfort to the family. He continues to frequently remind them, "You can miss Jim a little bit, but don't be sad. Remember what the angel said, that Jim is happy and healthy in heaven, and he doesn't want you to be sad."

Stevie, in his unassuming child-like faith has brought much peace and healing to Jeannie and her family. Truly, God, in His compassion, reached out to them at a time of deep sorrow and heartache with reassuring words of hope and comfort through Stevie's encounter with the angel.

"Blessed are those who mourn for they shall be comforted," (Mt. 5:4). What a creative way God used to comfort a family in their time of grief.

Two Questions

Earlier, I mentioned that a vision or dream, like any word from God, must stand two tests. Who gets the glory and what is the fruit? Clearly, in each of these stories, God received the glory and there was much fruit as well. Briefly, for example, in the story about the trip to Europe, I was thankful for the reminder God gave me to step through the doors He initiates. Through that experience, the fruit was a deeper faith. Dennis gave jubilant praise and thanks to God for His healing and his faith also grew immeasurably. Again, God was acknowledged in Stevie's angelic vision which exhibited the fruit of comfort, hope and peace in the family as they grieved the loss of Jim.

Master's Degree

I can't end this chapter without mentioning another kind of dream that God gives to many people. Sometimes, God places a desire in our heart to accomplish something. This can also be a dream, not one that comes while we are asleep, but one that sparks a fire in our heart, one that beckons and summons us to move forward with a plan. Sometimes, God places a unique call on our lives, one that we long to see accomplished. It burns in our heart, and we sense a passion and zeal for the dream to be realized, to come to fruition.

Often with the dream, however, there comes a period of waiting. I sometimes think God enjoys having us wait for things. Maybe you have noticed that in your life, too. I can't get past the exhortation over and over in the Bible that tells us to "wait for the Lord." Here are just a few verses.

> Psalm 27:14 *"**Wait** for the Lord; Be strong and let your heart take courage; Yes, wait for the Lord."*

> Psalm 37:7 *"Rest in the Lord and **wait** patiently for Him...."*

> Psalm 37:34 *"**Wait** for the Lord and keep His way...."*

> Psalm 62:1 *"My soul **waits** in silence for God only...."*

> Psalm 130:5 *"I **wait** for the Lord, my soul does wait, and in His word do I hope."*

> Psalm 147:11 *"The Lord favors those who fear Him, Those who **wait** for His lovingkindness."*

> Micah 7:7 *"But as for me, I will watch expectantly for the Lord; I will **wait** for the God of my salvation. My God will hear me."*

Are you getting the idea? God is into waiting. I think He likes that concept. He had me wait thirty years for a desire He had placed in my heart as a young woman. When God is the one who puts a desire or a dream in our heart, you can be sure He will, in time, give opportunity for it to be accomplished. You see, God is personally invested in our dreams. If they are from Him, He will eventually open doors. Of course, we have to cooperate and move forward with the dream when the time is right. He initiates and we follow.

*"I will cry to God Most High... who accomplishes all
things for me"* (Ps. 57:2).

"The Lord will accomplish what concerns me..." (Ps.
138:8).

*"My purpose will be established and I will accomplish
all My good pleasure"* (Isa. 46:10).

For thirty years, I had longed to go back to school for a Master's
degree in Biblical Studies. I had earned a Bachelor of Science in
Elementary Education after high school and had taught school for
a couple years before starting our family. In those days, a pregnant
woman was not allowed to teach, so my career ended quickly. Two
years later, I became a Christian, mostly out of desperation for
meaning and purpose in life. Two more years passed, and during that
time the Lord's call on my life to teach the Bible was firmly planted.
I have been teaching the Bible for the past forty-five years. With the
joy of finding my place of ministry, I longed to further my personal
understanding of God's word by going back to school for a graduate
degree in Biblical Studies.

I began to look for a school to accomplish that goal but found
frustration at every turn. We lived in a small Midwest town where
the closest seminary was almost two hours away. The cost was
exorbitant, and Bill was not supportive of the idea. We had children
to raise, and I was needed at home.

Although I agreed it was not the right timing, the desire God had
placed in my heart did not diminish over the years. At times, I would
approach Bill. "Is this the right time yet?" to which he would answer,
"No, I don't think so." His answer was always the same... "not yet."

More than once, I felt discouraged and pleaded with the Lord, *if
this dream is not from you, then please remove the desire.* One year,
I even made the choice to die to my dream, to put it on the altar and
leave it there. What use was it to continue to want something that
didn't seem like it would ever happen? *Not my will but Thine be done.*

That worked for awhile, but soon the longing to continue my education bubbled up again. Thirty years passed. During that time my family grew up, went to college, and all three married.

From the beginning, I had made the decision that I would not try to follow my dream without Bill's full support. I strongly believe that God honors a woman whose heart is submissive to her husband's counsel. So I waited...and waited...and waited.

The dream refused to die. After 30 years I again prayed, *Lord, I believe it is You who have placed this desire in my heart for a Master's degree. Bill has said no each time I have asked if it was right season yet. I have submitted to him each time, feeling that he prayed and had my best interest at heart. I'm getting older. It seems if I'm ever to accomplish this goal, it will have to be soon. I'm going to ask Bill one last time, and if he says "No" again, I will be done.*

I fervently prayed for two weeks before approaching Bill this last time. Finally, I gathered the courage. It was in God's hand to direct the answer. "Bill, you know I have wanted to go back to school for many years now. What do you think? Is it time yet?"

His answer took me completely off guard. "Yes, I think it is," he casually replied. So casually, I thought I had misheard him. "What did you say?" I asked in disbelief.

"Yes, Betsy, but I think you should get a job for a season and earn at least part of the tuition. People appreciate things more when they have personally invested in them. Then, you will need to go online and find a school."

That week, I drove up to the local high school, applied for and was offered a part-time job in the guidance department. I worked there for a year. By then, graduate schools offered online classes, and God led me to a seminary that looked like a perfect fit for the kind of classes I wanted. I decided to only take one class at a time, completing three per year, so as not to interfere with any of our "post children" activities. It took me four glorious years to complete my studies, and I savored every moment. More than once, I prayed Bible teacher, Beth Moore's, prayer. *Lord, make me smarter than I am.*

To this day, I'm not sure exactly why God put the longing in my heart for a Master's degree. By the time I graduated I was too old to teach at the college level. I continue to teach home and church Bible studies. Maybe God just wanted to bless me with something that fit who He had created me to be. Maybe it was just the journey to get there and the life lessons I learned along the way. Maybe it's not for here but for the hereafter.

I may never know why, but I do know that God met me in a very special way when He fulfilled the desire He had placed in my heart. I cherished every moment I got to study. I loved every class. I thoroughly enjoyed every paper I was privileged to write, and God prepared me for every exam. The overall experience was stellar. Maybe, I appreciated it so much because I had to wait so long for it.

Bill says, "When a person gets a doctorate, he's called a doctor. What do you call a person who gets a master's? No, Betsy, I will not call you Master," but he loves to tease me regularly by calling me Dr. Betsy. Actually, I don't mind.

Study Guide 7

1. A. What two ways of receiving a word from God are mentioned in Acts 2:17?
   B. Define vision.

   C. Define dream.

2. What is their purpose?

3. A. Joseph, the Cupbearer, the Baker, and Pharaoh had dreams in Genesis 37-41.
   Pick one of their dreams and tell about it here.

   B. What was the outcome of their dreams?

4. Recall the experience of another biblical character who had a vision or a dream.

5. A. Why is it important to let God take the initiative in giving visions and dreams rather than seeking them ourselves?

   B. What two questions can we ask to be sure a vision or dream is from God?

6. Can you share a time God spoke to you through a vision or dream? If not, share how you responded to the dreams mentioned in this chapter.

CHAPTER 8

God Speaks Through His Creation

"The heavens are telling of the glory of God... (Ps. 19:1).

A Voice Without Words

HEARING GOD'S VOICE through creation is a unique experience in that it is a voice without words. Nature surely speaks loudly of the beauty of the Lord, His majesty, His awesome power, His creativity. It can also articulate rich lessons about life. There is an enigma in that, while there is no actual voice, the message can be quite clear, and at times, dramatic. Who hasn't looked up at a starry sky, even observed a speck in the night sky called Mars, and not been in awe of God's power and magnificence. Or, who hasn't walked along a quiet forest path and been aware of His order and peace?

If you have ever been captivated by the otherworldly appearance of Bryce Canyon in Utah, inspired by the glory of the Rocky Mountains of Colorado, or stunned at the magnitude of the Grand Canyon, you understand the splendor of God's creation. Who could miss His thunderous, commanding voice at Niagara Falls? *"The voice of the Lord is powerful. The voice of the Lord is majestic"* (Ps. 29:4)

One has only to observe the brilliant colors of birds and flowers in Hawaii, experience a dazzling sunset over the ocean, or be astounded by the massive roar of a thunder storm to realize that God speaks of His grandeur and manifests Himself in a powerful way through nature. Consider the uniqueness of the animals He has created. The supremacy and incomparable beauty of His extraordinary innovations, as expressed in His creativity, loudly proclaim who He is.

Job 12:7-10 articulates it well: *"But now ask the beasts, and let them teach you; and the birds of the heavens, and let them tell you. Or speak to the earth, and let it teach you; And let the fish of the sea declare to you. Who among all these does not know that the hand of the Lord has done this? In whose hand is the life of every living thing and the breath of all mankind?"*

The Tiny Bouquet

The flowers of God's creation can hold special lessons if we fine tune our attention to observe them. When we were backpacking with friends in the High Sierras of California, we decided to climb to the top of one of the lower peaks near East Lake. A beautiful, sunny day provided us the opportunity to be still and know that He is God. As we quietly drank in the splendor of the panoramic view, we all contemplated the awesomeness of God. Truly, He is to be exalted.

Glancing down, amidst gigantic rock formations, I noticed, there in a rocky crag, hardly noticeable to the casual eye, the tiniest, most delicate spray of sunny yellow wildflowers. God had placed this beautiful bouquet in this remote location, unseen by most people on planet earth. My eyes, in their rush to take in the glory of the expanse surrounding us, had almost bypassed this breathtaking splash of color. How could such a lovely cluster of flowers exist so high above sea level, here in the crevice of a rock?

As I pondered the beauty around me and this simple, delicate patch of flowers, God spoke to me from Matthew 6:29-30. *"Yet I say to you that even Solomon in all his glory did not clothe himself like one of these. But if God so arrays the grass of the field, which is alive today and tomorrow is thrown into the furnace, will He not much more do so for you, O men of little faith?"*

I was struck with a fresh realization of God's deep, abiding concern and commitment to me and to all His people. I felt His comfort and assurance. If He cared for the tiniest flowers, whose beauty I may have been the only human to behold, surely He cared about me.

I considered how often in the hurriedness of life, we overlook the small treasures God has placed in our paths. In our busyness going here and there, we can run right by the matchless beauty of God's creation. This fragile floral arrangement was a reminder to slow down, delight in, and appreciate God's wonderful creativity.

As I continued to apply the truth of this encounter, I wondered how many missed relationships or by-passed opportunities also go unnoticed as we rush through each day. Often, we find ourselves consumed with the urgent at the expense of the important things in life. I was reminded to take time to smell the roses, to observe the wonder of God's workmanship around me, to take time for people, to be aware of their needs. Yes, God can speak through the vast expanses of His creation and even through the most delicate flowers.

Colorado River

I love hiking trails, rivers, waterfalls, and especially the mountains of Colorado. I especially enjoy how God speaks to me on our various road trips. As we wandered along the highway next to the Colorado River one year, the Lord revealed a clear lesson. For many miles, I observed the dynamics of this spirited, energetic river. Dashing over rocks and boulders, this massive flow of water raged undaunted past anything in its path. Sometimes, only small rocks blocked the way. Glistening, white spray was the only visible evidence that the river had collided with anything. Other times, the water impacted large boulders as it hastened toward its destination, sending up a violent, crashing surge of foam as though proclaiming, "Do not mess with me!" These class five rapids spewing white water gave the only evidence of obstruction. Yet, nothing stopped the flow. Charging at accelerated speed through its channel, the river relentlessly followed the passageway carved out before it.

Whatever the opposition, the river coursed onward, single-minded in purpose as it hastened toward the ocean. No obstacle was big enough to bring the river to a halt. Water either surged over the tops of rocks or cut a path around them, eventually wearing them down, always finding a way to continue its journey.

As I watched this interesting phenomenon, a Bible verse came to mind and the Lord began to speak a lesson to me. *"No temptation has overtaken you but such as is common to man; and God is faithful, who will not allow you to be tempted beyond what you are able, but with the temptation will provide the way of escape also, that you may be able to endure it"* (I Cor. 10:13).

Pondering that verse, I began to see that the rocks and boulders in the Colorado River were like the temptations and trials we have in life. A way of escape always materialized for the water, either around the rocks or over them. Single-minded, the water flowed onward to the sea. In the same way, God promises to provide a way of escape for us. He is a faithful God who can be trusted. As we focus on the Lord, walking in His will as our destination, He faithfully provides whatever escape we need around the rocks and boulders in our lives. I felt comforted by the river and the message God gave me.

"He who believes in Me, as the Scripture said, 'From his innermost being will flow rivers of living water.' By this He spoke of the Spirit..." (Jn. 7:38-39).

Aspen Trees

As we have traveled through the mountains of Colorado, we have been particularly fascinated with Aspen trees and their shimmering, silvery leaves as they glistened in the sun. Aspens are unique trees for more than just their leaves, however.

As I studied to speak at a banquet one year, I was struck by some interesting facts about Aspens and how the Lord spoke some practical lessons to me concerning them. For instance, did you know that Aspen trees grow in groves and share a common root system? You won't find any lone Aspens. They are always in community. Each tree can live forty to one hundred and fifty years, but the root system of the colony lives much longer. The individual trees are actually born from a single, interconnected root system that dates back thousands of years. They are attached to each other deep underground. Because they are so deeply rooted, they have a destiny that continually produces more trees of their kind.

While forest fires can be devastating to most kinds of trees, they are beneficial to the Aspen colony. Because of their common root deep below the heat of the flame, Aspens are able to survive forest fires. Fire only burns out the old trees, allowing for growth in the root system. In time, soon after the fire burns out, new sprouts begin to grow.

As I studied the interesting aspects of Aspen trees, I began to see parallels with Christian principles. When this kind of prompting happens, I believe it is God speaking to me. The first object lesson I saw was that just as Aspen trees grow from a shared root, so do we as Christians share the same root, Jesus Christ, and it is in Him that we enjoy growth.

As Bill taught a Sunday school lesson one Sunday, he asked the question, "Why is a tree able to stand upright?"

The obvious answer came quickly as one student offered, "The stability of the root system allows the tree to stand."

"We could say then," Bill added, "that in like manner, we are established and have the ability to stand firm in our lives as our roots go deep into the Lord."

I was reminded of Colossians 2:7 *"having been firmly rooted and now being built up in Him and established in your faith...."* Aspen trees share a close knit family unit in any given grove because they are all dependent on the same root system. In like manner we, as the family of God, are to be there for one another.

Another lesson regarding the idea of new growth from Aspen forest fires is that there are also times in our lives when we may endure a fiery experience. In like manner, God often uses trials in our lives to burn out areas that hinder our growth. He then blesses us with fresh, new increase. He builds our character and faith through the difficulties we encounter. Because we are attached to the strong root of Jesus Christ, we are not destroyed in times of trial.

The Tree Outside My Window

While on the subject of trees, I'm reminded of another tree that God used to instruct me, a tree outside my upstairs office window. Light enters the room through one small window. When sitting at my desk looking up, I see only the sky and the tops of several large, stately trees in our neighbor's yard. As the seasons go by, I observe the leaves as they bud, blossom, turn color, and eventually fall to the ground.

In the winter, I watch as the snow beats against the bare branches. When the sun shines, I observe shadows playing on the leaves. On stormy days, I notice the rain dripping from the limbs. On gusty days, I see the wind's effects as the branches toss to and fro, the leaves twisting and turning.

One evening, while praying, I glanced up at the window and my eyes met with darkness. Nothing visible penetrated the blackness of night, not even the hint of a shadow or vague form of a tree. While I knew the trees were still out there and their branches were waving in the wind, the darkness of the night had obscured and hidden them. I could only see darkness.

God impressed me with a nugget of truth through this picture from my window. The scene depicted the way life is at times when we look out and only see darkness, when life appears bleak and desolate. Circumstances or relationships may look discouraging and hopeless. We seek God but don't sense His presence.

Distraught, we may feel God has forgotten us. Pain and frustration permit only a vision of darkness, the absence of light. Sometimes, perspective in a situation evades us. Lacking understanding, we may become confused and frustrated. As we grope in the darkness, we begin to question God's presence. Yet, even in these dark times, we can know that God is still there. He remains alive and well, accomplishing His purposes.

Just because I couldn't see the trees didn't mean they had left. In reality, they still waved their branches in the wind. We need to remember that darkness is temporary, sometimes part of God's plan while He works in the background. Just as I could trust that the trees would still be there in the morning, God can be trusted to be there when we don't see Him or sense His presence, when we're unaware of His nearness. This is part of the wonder of what faith brings into our lives.

God speaks through His creation all around us, and if we tune in, there are lessons to learn. If you are in a difficult situation, I hope you find encouragement in knowing He is always there.

The Webbed Tree

We had another interesting tree experience involving a small flowering tree between our neighbor's house and ours. One spring, it produced its leaves as usual, but then something strange began to happen. We noticed that something was eating the tree. Upon closer observation, we saw that a type of worm had not only eaten the leaves but had covered the tree with a coat of gray webbing. Within a week, every leaf on the tree was gone, replaced by thick, gray, hanging webs which covered the trunk and every branch. It looked like something out of a horror movie.

Disturbed by this sudden vicious attack on the tree, we called in several plant authorities to look at it. Other trees were also under attack, and we envisioned our entire yard being devoured. To our dismay, no one had any idea what kind of worm was consuming the trees.

We, and our neighbors, assumed the tree would die as a result of the assault, but decided not to cut it down right away. We sprayed it and waited. Gruesome though it was, looking stripped and dead, we gradually accepted that we would have to look at this macabre sight for months to come. It became a conversation piece for all visitors.

About a month later, upon inspection, we noticed a hint of green inching forth from the limbs. Incredibly, over the next few weeks, the tree completely re-leafed and shed all of the webbing. Eventually, to the casual onlooker, there remained no sign that anything had ever been wrong.

As I pondered the remarkable recovery of this tree, God began to speak. This tree represented His work in the life of a believer. There are things that eat away at our lives - disturbing relationships, unresolved problems, emotional upheaval. We come to a point where we feel we have been completely stripped of our resources. We feel there's nothing left, so what's the use? The proverbial worm has eaten away all the green. We are bereft of any help or solution. We feel we are at the end of our rope, lost, helpless, and maybe even hopeless. Then, ever so gradually, as we trust God, a change begins to occur. At first, just a hint of new growth surfaces, but as time passes, soon we stand in full leaf having shorn all the gray webbing of doubt, confusion, and fear that had entangled our branches.

We can know that Jesus is Lord even in the most seemingly hopeless situations. When the worm has done its final damage and all looks futile, that's the time to look up and begin watching for the first signs of fresh growth. God grows us best when we run out of resources.

Perhaps you have noticed a theme that is evident in the three stories about trees. Each story held a similar lesson, and the lesson flowed into one theme. God cares. He is there during our trials. He wants us to be rooted in Him so that when the dark times come, we are anchored. Trees are a picture of seasons, a promise of new growth, a symbol of hope. God can use even trees to speak to us with instruction and understanding.

Beauty from Fire

Another occasion when God reminded me of His presence and bigger plan in trials involved fires in California. Grass fires occur annually in many parts of California. An interesting phenomenon manifests as a result of some of these fires. After the burning has spent its rage, the only remains are charred trees and the blackened ash of what used to be golden grasses. For months, the hills remain barren and unproductive, but with the first rains in the fall, something begins to happen.

God has created a special flower in some parts of California, that only germinates every forty or fifty years and only after a fire. The seeds, implanted in the ground, remain dormant for years until the heat of a fire stirs them to growth. The unique flowers that result are worth the wait as they burst forth in a brilliant, dazzling, orange shade. Against the blackened landscape, their presence displays a magnificent tribute to the glory of God.

Aware of these beautiful flowers one day, God spoke to me. In His quiet way, my thoughts considered that sometimes God allows us to endure a trial or fiery ordeal that burns many things out of our heart. At the time, we may feel charred and barren, but God never stops there. His purpose is to bring out the beauty, to redeem and restore. Only God knows hidden areas of loveliness that have been dormant for many years, just like the flowers in California.

As a fiery test chafes at our character, burning out impurities, we can know that God's ultimate purpose is to draw out the splendor of a vibrant flower in the end. Some of God's most inwardly beautiful and sensitive people are those who have been tested by fire and come again into bloom and prosperity.

Nature in the Bible

Let's pause for a moment and remind ourselves of verses in the Bible that use aspects of God's creation to speak to us. God incorporates many word pictures and parables to describe spiritual principles. Being a good communicator, He brings examples of common things, often from nature, to remind us of various truths. There are hundreds of such verses from which to choose. I'm reminded of John 15:5 where Jesus says, *"I am the vine, you are the branches; he who abides in Me and I in him, he bears much fruit, for apart from Me you can do nothing."* Vines, branches, fruit, all part of

God's creation. Such a clear reference as Jesus reveals that the way to bear spiritual fruit is to abide in Him.

Proverbs 30:25 articulates a lesson to be learned from ants and how they prepare their food in the summer. The Bible has lessons about how God cares even about the sparrow, how we are to be cautioned by sheep in wolf's clothing. Pigs, oxen, cattle, locusts, eagles, and scorpions are among the vast menagerie of animal life calling us to their lessons. Jesus is called the Lion of Judah, a picture of strength and confidence. Each of these examples has the potential to be a personal word at an appropriate moment.

Psalm 1:3 illustrates what those who trust God will be like. *"He will be like a tree firmly planted by streams of water, which yields its fruit in its season and its leaf does not wither; and in whatever he does, he prospers."* Here is a clear word from God using things from nature: a tree, streams of water, fruit, and leaves. God is speaking of the benefits available to a person who is firmly rooted and gathering strength and sustenance from Him.

We could go on with scores of examples from Scripture of how God speaks through His creation. They make powerful word pictures that form visuals in our mind. God knows that when we relate a principle to a picture, it becomes sharper, easier to grasp, and better remembered. Jesus' parables were spoken using this technique, and they are ageless in their effect.

In speaking to us through His creation, we have seen God use metaphors of trees, rivers, flowers, and even fire to reveal secret treasures in hidden places. Are we listening? Awareness is the first step to hearing God's voice.

In this next story, God, in His creative way, spoke to Jeannie through a dove and an eagle. You will see that if we are expecting God to speak through His creation, we can't miss it. Perhaps, her story will remind you of a time He spoke to you.

A Dove and an Eagle

Just before sunrise, on a cold and snowy day in February, I woke up feeling sad. My beloved husband, Jim, had passed away a little over a year ago. Mornings seemed to be the most difficult time for me. Jim was always up early, full of energy, enjoying the sunrise over the lake, eager to get to his business.

Now, as I sat alone, I opened my Bible for devotions and began to pray for peace and comfort. A scripture that I had memorized as a child came to my mind. *"And the peace of God, which passeth all understanding, shall keep your hearts and minds through Christ Jesus"* (Phil. 4:7 KJV).

As I opened my eyes, I noticed a pink glow on the pages of my Bible. Turning to look out the window overlooking the lake, the most beautiful pink sunrise came into view. It was such a pristine morning. The ice and snow on the lake looked like sparkling pink diamonds.

Then, to my amazement, there was a mourning dove perched in a tree just outside my bedroom window. Tears welled up in my eyes as I thanked the Lord for a dove which is a symbol of peace and hope. I recalled that a dove is also associated with the spirit of the Lord since it was a dove that descended upon Jesus when He was baptized. Then, I also remembered another time a dove appeared in the Bible. Noah released a dove, which flew back triumphantly with an olive leaf. It brought reassurance that trees were growing on dry land - a certain sign of life.

I began to feel refreshed and comforted. God was speaking to me through the sighting of one of His creatures. It was more than coincidence. It was God reaching out to me in my time of mourning bringing a comfort that only He can provide.

But that wasn't all. Two days later, again at sunrise, I was feeling a little overwhelmed by all the estate issues and added responsibilities following my husband's death. This particular morning, I prayed for strength and wisdom and began to claim God's promise that *"...They that wait upon the Lord shall renew their strength. They shall mount up with wings as eagles, they shall run and not be weary, they shall walk and not faint"* (Isa. 40:31).

When I finished my prayer, I glanced outside to see the softly falling snow and was totally amazed to see an eagle perched in a snow covered tree right outside my window. I watched it for a few minutes and then, it spread it wings and flew majestically toward the sunrise. What a visual encouragement God brought that He would renew my strength that day, just as with the eagle.

What an awesome God! I'm so blessed by God's reminders that He is the creator of all things. I love how he speaks peace, strength and hope through his Word, beautiful sunrises and birds. Even as I am writing this on a bright and sunny morning in March, there is a gold finch chirping a song for me. I believe it is saying... *"O Lord, our Lord, how majestic is your name in all the earth"* (Ps. 8:9).

Tomato Lesson

Continuing with lessons from God's creation, I will tell you about my experience gardening. One particular spring, our neighbor chopped down a large maple tree located between our yards. Although I love trees, the elimination of this one was to our benefit as it left our yard with a longed for sunny area. Due to many trees on our property, previously, we did not have a sunny place to plant a garden. With the removal of this one tree now, Bill decided to build me a raised garden which he filled with dirt. It measured about four feet by eight.

At first, my mind went overboard, and I imagined my garden filled with all kinds of vegetables and herbs. In the end, I decided to start small and see how I would do with a few tomato plants. By a few, I mean twelve. Well, after all, when I bought them, the plants were tiny, so twelve sounded small. I could only find four wire cages in the garage to prop them on, so I put two plants inside each one. The rest would just have to be propped up by a stick.

Faithfully, I watered and fertilized. As the plants grew larger, I watched expectantly each week for the little flowers and then small green tomatoes to appear on the vines. At first, only a few appeared and then, suddenly, the plants seemed to explode with tomatoes, all turning red at once. *What would I do with so many? I know. I'll give them away.* With that decision, I began to experience the joy not only of sowing and reaping, but of giving out of abundance.

From this gardening experience, I noticed that I could give away dozens of tomatoes and in a few short days be rewarded with dozens more, ripe on the vine, ready for eating. I quickly realized that being given abundance was for the purpose of sharing with others and reaping the joy of doing so.

The Bible expresses it this way, *"Give, and it will be given to you. They will pour into your lap a good measure, pressed down, shaken together, and running over. For by your standard of measure it will be measured to you in return"* (Lk. 6:38).

That summer and in others, we have had plenty of tomatoes on our own table, and more than once, had plenty to share with others. It was fun experiencing the appreciation of others as I presented them with a bag full of fresh, home grown tomatoes.

Isn't this principle true in all things in life? God spoke to me that what we give away has a way of coming back to us so that we can give more away. It is a principle begging to be tried in a number of areas of life. We cannot out-give God, whether it's in the financial realm, or just tomatoes. He always catches up with a blessing.

More on Tomatoes

During the growing season of my tomato plants, there were other things I became aware of that proffered parallel spiritual lessons as God spoke them to me. For instance, I mentioned previously that I had bought twelve plants and planted them by twos. This seemed prudent at the start because they were so small. But as you may know, tomato plants can become quite large and gangly. Having two in each wire cage made it impossible to keep the sprawling branches in their proper place. Like undisciplined children, they insisted on spreading out in every possible direction with no logic, planning, or efficiency in their quest for space. All of my efforts to train them where to grow were in vain. They stretched out and lopped their tomatoes down at will.

In my little garden, I soon ventured out by planting green and red peppers, sweet basil, rosemary, green beans, zucchini, and cucumbers. One evening before dinner, Bill went out to the garden to pick some basil for me. Time passed, and I wondered what was taking him so long. Returning, he commented that he could not find the basil plant. Impossible, I thought. It was there last week, tall and thriving. I followed him out, confident it would be in plain sight, but upon searching the garden, I could not find it either. Where it had been was now overrun with tomato branches. Underneath several heavily laden vines, I finally located my basil plant. It seemed to be gasping for air. If it could have talked, I'm sure it would have demanded that I find a more suitable location for it to grow.

Jesus often used gardening as a means of articulating a particular truth. Many, in His day, were farmers and could easily relate to his stories. I wonder what lessons He would have wanted me to glean from my experience of garden overgrowth. Perhaps, the lesson was just a reminder that too many good things can crowd out the important things in life. Possibly, He was prompting me to recall that it is easy for life to become congested. Maybe, He just wanted to remind me to plant fewer vegetables and herbs next time and to plant them farther apart.

The Best Kind of Snow

In Michigan, while summers are hot and muggy, perfect for growing my garden, one winter evening, as I looked out my office window, I noticed that we had about six inches of snow from our latest winter storm, and it was the best kind of snow. It jogged my memory back to several years before as I remembered well a snow like this one. It started falling around dinner time. Like soft powder, it accumulated quickly to eight or ten inches or more. Every winter, I wait for this kind of snow which only happens a few times each season. That night after dinner, I bundled up in my wool scarf, gloves, boots, and jacket. Pulling up my hood, I drew the drawstrings tight. It was only twenty degrees outside, but I could not resist being part of this sparkling wonderland.

Walking cautiously across the garage to the driveway, my boots slid in the mounting snow. I grabbed the snow shovel and proceeded with the task of clearing the glistening driveway. Logic told me that if I succeeded in clearing the present eight inches, we might be able to drive out of the driveway in the morning. However, the snow was coming so fast that another couple inches accumulated before I could finish.

As I started back to the warmth of our home, a thought surfaced in my mind. *You haven't been cross country skiing for several years. This is perfect snow and the streets haven't yet been cleared. You are sixty-three years old. What if this is the last year that you ever ski?* As you may have guessed, eight inches of powder beckoned me, called to me, but it was late, I reasoned, almost 10:00 P.M. *Should I do this? Why not?*

Quickly heading to the basement, if I remembered correctly, the cross country skis should still be in the storeroom. Ah, yes, there they were propped up against the wall. But where were the ski poles? Rummaging through some old curtain rods and boards stacked in a corner, I untangled them from their hiding place. Perfect! Brushing off years of collected dust, I fumbled to carry my awkward load upstairs.

Slipping on an extra pair of socks and my ski shoes, I was set to go. Gathering my skis, I clumsily stepped out through the garage to the breathtaking, spectacular world of crystalline white that awaited me.

Click, click went the locks as I set the shoes onto the skis. I was ready, one foot in front of the other, gliding down the driveway. Crunch, swish, crunch, swish, marking the trail, as I lifted each foot in and out of the fine sea of snow. Up to the corner of our street, I glided, then tracing my ski tracks, back to the driveway. Snow gathered on my coat and boots, and swirled around my face. *Wow...I can still do it. This is exhilarating.* My breathing increased as I inhaled the cold, crisp air. This is what it means to live in the moment, stepping out of the ordinary and being impetuous. It is part of the

Betsy Tacchella

thrill of winter in Michigan, but how did God use this experience to speak to me?

I believe, in part, God was showing me this is how He meant me to live, maybe not always, but at times, spontaneously, moment by moment, always taking my cue from Him, listening to His voice, following His lead, unafraid of trying something new or retrying something old. We can glory in Him as we appreciate His beauty, the splendor of a quiet, shimmering, snowy night, childlike in response. This was a night of joy, a night of sheer delight, living in the moment, enjoying God's beauty and his endless creativity. *"You will make known to me the path of life; In Your presence is fullness of joy; In Your right hand there are pleasures forever"* (Ps. 16:11).

His Voice in the Heavens

Speaking of God's creativity, we can't leave this chapter without including what is seen when we look upward. Isaiah 40:26 encourages us to lift our eyes to the heavens. *"Lift up your eyes on high and see who has created these stars, the One who leads forth their host by number, He calls them all by name; Because of the greatness of His might and the strength of His power, not one of them is missing."*

Astronomers claim there are over forty sextillion stars. Written out, that number would look like this: 40,000,000,000,000,000,000,000. That is a lot of stars, billions more than our finite minds can comprehend. Interestingly, God has counted each one, not only counted them, but given them each a name. Orion, Pleiades, and Mazzaroth are a few names mentioned in Scripture.

"He counts the number of the stars; He gives names to all of them. Great is our Lord, and abundant in strength. His understanding is infinite" (Ps. 147:4, 5).

Louis Giglio has an amazing video series found on youtube called "How Great is Our God," where he speaks about galaxies, stars, planets, and other phenomenal creations by the Mastermind of the universe. As you watch, you will hear God's voice loud and clear. He will say things to you about how great and awesome He is, and how spectacular is the work of His hands, His creation. Your image of God will vastly increase as you consider the breathtaking splendor and grandeur of what He has prepared in the heavens. There are no words magnificent enough to explain who He is. As you take in the glory of God in the heavens, you may want to stop and worship Him. As I watched the video, I certainly did. I stand in wonder and awe as I take in the majesty of His creation.

One worship song I enjoy speaks of Him as holy, wonderful, marvelous, glorious, omnipotent, righteous, and mighty. That just scratches the surface, but that automatic response of worship is truly God speaking to stir our hearts to fall to our knees in praise of who He is and what He does.

You will also better understand Psalm 19:1-4. *"The heavens are telling of the glory of God; And their expanse is declaring the work of His hands. Day to day pours forth speech, and night to night reveals knowledge. There is no speech, nor are there words; Their voice is not heard. Their line has gone out through all the earth, and their utterances to the end of the world. In them He has placed a tent for the sun."*

It seems like an oxymoron to think that the heavens pour forth speech, yet, at the same time, their voice is not heard. Truly, the heavens do speak loudly of the glory of God, but it is not through verbal communication. If we take the time to listen to God speak through His creation, we will know we have heard Him when we find ourselves responding with worship.

As you have seen or heard in this chapter, God can speak to us through His creation. He may have a lesson through either word pictures or real events and may use anything we encounter in our environment. Whether it is a lesson from the animal kingdom, the plant kingdom, astronomy, landscape scenery or other things in the His world of nature, God can use it all to reveal more of Himself and speak into our lives. Our God is an awesome God worthy of our worship.

Study Guide 8

1. Did any of the stories in this chapter speak to you personally? Explain how.

2. Find a verse for each of these words in your Bible. Make observations about your verses as to what God is saying to you.

   A. Trees

   B. Flowers

   C. Rivers

   D. Water

   E. Stars

3. Why do you think God uses object lessons from nature?

4. What does this tell you about God?

5. Share a time God spoke to you through nature.

CHAPTER 9

How to be Sure It is God's Voice

"My sheep hear My voice, and I know them, and they follow Me" (John 10:27).

Four Guidelines

IN THIS SECTION, I would like to pause a moment and share four guidelines that can help us stay on track when we think we have heard a rhema word, a personal word from God, especially in regard to direction. With so many other voices vying for our attention, it is important to make sure it is God we are hearing. Over the years, I have personally found that if all four of these guidelines are in sync, there is a better probability that the word is from God. However, if not, I consider it a yellow light of caution telling me to wait. Further confirmation may be warranted before proceeding. Possibly, the timing may not be right.

As you read this list, you may want to hold an area of your life up to it. Perhaps, you feel you have heard from God concerning a situation in your life. Why not start now to use these four guidelines which are four questions we can ask ourselves:

1. **Does the rhema word line up with the Bible and with the character of Christ?** *"Your word is a lamp to my feet and a light to my path,"* (Ps. 119:105).
2. **Do I have peace of mind?** *"And the peace of God, which surpasses all comprehension, will guard your hearts and your minds in Christ Jesus,"* (Phil. 4:7).
3. **Do the circumstances fit?** *"Like apples of gold in settings of silver is a word spoken in right circumstances,"* (Pr. 25:11).
4. **Do I have confirmation from other believers?** *"Every fact is to be confirmed by the testimony of two or three witnesses,"* (II Cor.13:1).

Let's look more closely at each of these areas to see how they help in deciding whether we have heard God's voice.

Lining Up With the Bible and the Character of Christ

Clearly, our most important guideline is making sure that every word we think we hear from God must stand up to the ultimate test of Scripture. There are many decisions in life that will not have a specific verse defining exactly what to do, but there are overriding principles that can be considered in evaluating how to proceed in making choices.

Perhaps you have heard of the man who was debating what to do with his life. He randomly opened his Bible to a verse that said in part, *"And Judas went away and hanged himself."*

Not sure this instruction applied to him, the man looked for another random verse and found this partial text, *"Go thou and do likewise."* Still uncertain, a third time he chanced on one additional verse, *"What thou doeth, do quickly."*

Clearly, this haphazard approach to Scripture can lead to a conclusion which is neither biblical nor wise. That is why determining if the word also aligns with the character of Christ is important. You can see how knowing the Bible and its intent is as vital as knowing the character of our Lord when determining a rhema word. The two are inseparable.

You may know people who have twisted both a verse and what they claim to have heard from God in order to suit their own personal desires. Some try to justify their actions by finding a remote verse or a partial verse out of context. I recall a college graduation we attended where the speaker represented a popular secular news magazine. Because he was speaking at a Christian college, I suppose he felt he needed to incorporate a few Bible verses. One he chose was John 8:32, *"and you will know the truth, and the truth will make you free."* Truly, a wonderful verse, until we realized he was applying it to the media, specifically to the liberal magazine he represented. His out of context meaning was that if we read his magazine, we would know truth and it would set us free. Obviously, he failed to realize his magazine was not the truth this verse was referring to, if indeed, it was truth at all.

I have also talked to people who use the Bible to justify sin in their lives. They counter their immoral behavior with verses on love and compassion, insisting that their conduct is acceptable because they love the person. But again, this logic is not supported by Jesus' character. Clearly, if a person does not know the Bible well, it would be important to confirm the word with a mature Christian who is well versed in what God actually reveals as truth.

Peace of Mind

A second useful guideline is peace of mind. When God has spoken a word that lines up with the Bible and Jesus' character, we should experience an abiding peace. If a profound sense of unrest, confusion, or disorder continues with no sign of letting up, then it could be that the word is not from God. There should be an experience of inner tranquility and assurance, our heart at rest, and a sense of harmony with God. *"Thou wilt keep him in perfect peace, whose mind is stayed on thee: because he trusteth in thee"* (Isa. 26:3 KJV).

He will "*...guide our feet into the way of peace*" (Lk. 1:79). "*...Seek peace and pursue it*" (Ps. 34:14).

This does not mean that everything will necessarily come up roses, but even if the situation brings a measure of turmoil, there should still be a deep peace, a steadfast sense of rest, and a certain knowing that we are in the center of God's will.

It must be stressed that the peace factor, when making a decision, must be clearly attuned with the first principle, Scripture. Peace of mind by itself is simply an emotion that can be used to justify our own desires. It is possible to fool ourselves with a "feeling" of peace without consideration of the mind of Christ.

There are times when a word may leave us with an uncomfortable feeling, perhaps a slight dread regarding the unknown. This is not to be confused with an utter lack of inner peace. On the other hand, if the word continues to cause deep anxiety, then wait before acting or consider whether to abandon the idea altogether. A check in our spirit suggests that something isn't quite right. Perhaps, we can't even put our finger on what's wrong but we know we do not feel at ease with the word. Such an occasion arose for us as we considered sending our daughters to a Christian school.

Our girls were attending a public grade school. We loved our small, safe neighborhood school and were satisfied with their education and the caring atmosphere of the school. But one year, many of our friends transferred their children to a local Christian school. While we were not upset with public education, we, too, began to consider this idea. After all, we wanted the best for our girls. The Christian school offered excellence in academics plus an opportunity for children to be nurtured in the things of faith. It sounded ideal.

Setting up an appointment with the principal of the Christian school, our enthusiasm grew as we contemplated this potential change. Touring the school, we loved what we saw. The teachers displayed care and warmth. Quiet obedience, orderliness, and respect stood out as the norm in each classroom and the children appeared happy.

We filled out the application and proceeded with an interview. The girls passed the entrance test and we felt we could afford the school. Everything seemed to fall into place.

Still, one thing seemed strangely wrong. Though we liked the school, the pleasant atmosphere, the kind principal and teachers, and though they accepted the girls and we had the money, neither Bill nor I had peace. Everything seemed so right, but the more we prayed, the less peace we had.

We set up another interview with the principal. Surely another visit to the school would lighten our hearts. Although the appointment went well, we left with less peace than before. What could be wrong? Several weeks passed. During that time, whenever I thought of this school, turmoil mounted in my heart.

Wanting my guidelines to align before making a final decision, I asked God to give me a verse of Scripture to confirm His will in this matter. Since we had originally prayed about the school, we had felt God led us to go forward and pursue it. Now, we wondered if we had heard God or had just become swept up by the enthusiasm of our friends.

Finally, the day arrived when a decision had to be made. Again, I sat down with the Scriptures. *Lord, will you please show us your will for the girls?* My reading that day was in John 17. As my eyes came to verses 15-18, my heart leaped. I knew I was receiving a rhema word. *"I do not ask Thee to take them out of the world, but to keep them from the evil one. They are not of the world, even as I am not of the world. Sanctify them in the truth; Thy word is truth. As Thou didst send Me into the world, I also have sent them into the world"* (KJV).

That verse, coming to my attention at such a strategic time, became a sign that the girls were to be in the world but not of the world. I felt God wanted them to remain in the public school but not to conform to the ways of the world. This presented a unique challenge for us to take full responsibility to train the girls in truth. It would be up to us to filter the different ideas they would bring home and to hold them up to the light of biblical principles.

After confirming the word with Bill, I phoned the principal, thanked him for his kindness and declined enrolling the girls in the Christian school. Bill and I immediately felt at peace. We knew we had made the right decision for our family for that time.

It should be noted that several years later, under different circumstances, we did opt for a Christian school for Laurie one semester in Southern California. We hold Christian schools in the highest regard. Where parents choose to school their children remains a personal decision between each family and the Lord, whether public, Christian or home schooling. Peace of mind and the leading of the Holy Spirit should prevail as central factors when determining such an important issue.

Although lack of peace entered into our decision about whether to send the girls to a Christian school, a personal rhema word from the Scriptures was the final point that sealed the deal. For that situation, God chose to resolve our unrest with a verse from the Bible. Then, peace followed.

Circumstances That Fit

As we continue to look at guidelines, notice that each one ultimately rests on whether a rhema word lines up with Scripture. Under the next guideline, "Circumstances that Fit", you will also see that principle at work. When making a decision, there are usually several aspects to consider.

Bill had a situation where circumstances didn't quite line up. Having worked for the same company for many years, another company offered him a job that sounded wonderful. The new job would offer more independence and greater financial gain.

Although happy at his present job, the new opportunity looked attractive. Yet, as he considered the requirements for the position, circumstances became a serious consideration. The job would require many extra hours of work the first few years. That would mean time taken away from family and added stress on all of us. It also entailed large amounts of travel all over the United States that would further cut into family time. As Bill considered the opportunity, we all wondered if we would ever see him again.

After several months of prayerful pondering, he decided that no amount of financial or material gain could justify giving up his time at home. Bill had traveled a great deal early in our marriage, and it had not been conducive to family life. Ultimately, he felt his role in our home was more important. The circumstances surrounding this job offer did not line up with his goals for our family. He chose to turn down the offer.

There are many circumstances that come to our attention while making a decision. Weighing the positive and negative factors can help us decide whether we are hearing God's voice and moving toward His best plan.

While Bill was in the process of making his decision about the job offer, it was a biblical principle that eventually determined his answer. First Timothy 5:8 talks about the importance of providing for family. This verse goes beyond just financial provision. Bill knew that we needed his presence for emotional and spiritual support as well. The job in question would have frustrated both.

From these two examples, the Christian school decision and the job decision, we see that one guideline can be used to resolve another. For instance, we lacked peace about the school, but a Bible passage resolved the dilemma. As Bill considered the job offer, questionable circumstances had posed a problem. Aspects of the job did not line up with Bill's goals for our family. The biblical principle of the husband's role in providing for his family played a large part in that decision. Once the decision was made, we all felt at peace.

Confirmation from Other Believers

The fourth guideline in our list involves seeking confirmation from other believers. If a question arises about the validity of a word, it's prudent to bring it to the attention of two or three mature Christian friends or to a person in the role of spiritual authority. Other believers can sometimes help discern whether a word is valid.

Notice I said "mature Christian friends." I am specifically referring to believers who know God's Word. When we are looking for guidance with an issue, we will not necessarily receive biblical counsel from a non-Christian, a new Christian or an immature Christian friend. They may love you and want to help, but we cannot expect godly counsel from people who do not know God and His Word personally or from those for whom walking with God is a new experience. Many people have been led astray when a well meaning friend told them what they wanted to hear instead of what they needed to hear.

Counselors should be wise, respected, in the Word, willing to pray about the matter and willing to answer honestly. We need mentors who will speak the truth in love.

"...Every fact is to be confirmed by the testimony of two or three witnesses," (II Cor. 13:1). The word *fact* also translates from Greek rhema *word* in the King James Bible. The same definition applies here as applies to *word* in other places. A personal word from the Lord should stand the test of confirmation by other Christians, an accountability partner, a mentor, a pastor or other church leader.

We read a warning in Proverbs 11:14, *"Where there is no guidance, the people fall, but in abundance of counselors there is victory."* If there is a question about a word, it makes sense to seek godly counsel to see if it resonates with them. If moving in a certain direction doesn't seem appropriate to them, take their counsel seriously, wait before moving forward and, perhaps, revise your plan.

A dangerous thing happens in the body of Christ when we dogmatically say that the Lord has told us to do this or that. We are not meant to be lone rangers as Christians. Better to say, *I think the Lord is saying,* or *I feel the Lord might be telling me such and such.* Follow that up with, w*hat do you think?* This leaves a word open to be considered, prayed about and evaluated by others as to whether or not it is from the Lord. This principle is especially important regarding directional words from God.

Some Christians run into trouble when they resist confirmation by other believers. Christianity cannot be lived in a vacuum. We need each other. If we feel we have heard a word, it should stand the test of others reviewing it. If it doesn't, then we may need to pray and continue to seek God's direction.

A good way to incorporate other believers into decisions is to commit to involvement in a good church where biblical teaching is strong. Coming under the authority of the leadership of a Christ-centered church provides a safety net. When confused or unsure about how we perceive God's voice, God can use our local body of believers as a means to keep us on track. Scripture never encourages separation from the body of Christ because we need each other. Apart from a strong body of believers, we leave ourselves open to deception.

This is why it's important to select a church carefully, one that lifts up the name of Jesus, one where people are growing in knowledge and understanding of the Scriptures. To test whether a church is alive and thriving, several questions come to mind.

1. *Is there solid Bible teaching so that I'm growing in the Lord?*
2. *Are there opportunities and an open door for me to minister to others?*
3. *Is there strong, godly leadership that has a vision for the church?*

Of course, all these questions assume that we want to grow. It is possible to be in a good church and yet choose not to grow. However, if these areas are solidly in place, we can assume we are where God wants us to be until He directs otherwise. There are many voices calling for our attention. The Bible and the body of Christ both help to keep us on track.

Again, the four guidelines I've presented in this chapter usually work together: Lining up with the Bible and the character of Christ, peace of mind, circumstances that fit and confirmation from other believers. They are a team, and need to be properly aligned before taking action.

An Afterthought

There are many commands in the Bible that apply across the board to every believer. We do not need a rhema word to know that we should love our neighbor or to tell the truth. No personal word is necessary to know that we should forgive people who offend us. At the same time, it is important to note that there are events or ministries in our lives that require a specific word for our particular situation. A general word is not sufficient. Paul knew that the great commission from Jesus required going into all the earth to preach the gospel. That call, from Matthew 28:19, is a general summons to all believers to make disciples. If Paul had rushed out and traveled all over the world without receiving his specific mission from the Lord, however, he would have been far less effective.

In Acts 16:6-10, we know that God had not planned for Paul to speak the word in Asia at that time because the Holy Spirit forbade him to go there. We are not told exactly how He stopped him or why, but Paul got the message. Soon after though, he was prompted to travel to Macedonia. One word said to stop and another said to go.

"They passed through the Phrygian and Galatian region, having been forbidden by the Holy Spirit to speak the word in Asia and after they came to Mysia, they were trying to go into Bithynia, and the Spirit of Jesus did not permit them; and passing by Mysia, they came down to Troas. A vision appeared to Paul in the night: a man of Macedonia was standing and appealing to him, and saying, 'Come over to Macedonia and help us.' When he had seen the vision, immediately we sought to go into Macedonia, concluding that God had called us to preach the gospel to them."

The joy of hearing God's voice and the power that accompanied it, as he obeyed, brought forth much fruit in Paul's life and in the early church.

Goin' Fishing

A further example to help understand the importance of a rhema word for direction can be seen in Luke 5:5-7. In this story, Peter received a personal word from Jesus to let down the fishing nets. Peter had complained that he hadn't caught anything all night. As he obeyed the word, he quickly found his nets so full that they began to break. That's the way God builds faith. *"So faith comes from hearing and hearing by the (rhema) word of Christ"* (Rom. 10:17). Peter heard a word from Jesus, obeyed the word and saw an abundant provision. As a result, his faith increased.

Bill and our son enjoyed fishing trips when Mike was a young boy. However, I usually planned something else for dinner those evenings. They never came home with more than a few small fish, but they loved the sport and it was a great father-son bonding time.

What if they had claimed Peter's word for themselves? What if they had decided that since Peter's nets were filled, theirs would be too? Would they be filled? I'm afraid they might experience some disappointment. Why? They had not received a personal rhema word. There is no Christian doctrine entitled, *"Success in Fishing for All."*

Jesus also called Peter to walk on water as he was crossing the sea in his boat (Mt. 14:28-29). What if we also decided we could walk on water because Peter had? Obviously, we would be in for a wet surprise. If Peter's word had been a general word for the whole body of Christ, we would have a doctrine called *"Walking on Water,"* and everyone would engage in it. Unless we also receive a personal word to that extent, we had better stay in the boat.

Recognizing God's Voice

A speaker was once asked, "Do you mean God speaks to you in an audible voice?" To which he answered, "Oh, no, it's much louder than that!"

What does God's voice sound like when He speaks to us? Are there unique qualities about it? How will we recognize His voice?

Hearing God's voice should be a normal part of the Christian life. Like every other aspect of the Christian walk, hearing His voice requires faith.

When God speaks into our thoughts, we recognize it as a clear, distinct voice. It is not obscure, foggy or vague. Why? Because God is a God of light, not of darkness, a God of order, not confusion. When a word seems shadowy or ambiguous, dismiss it. In the Scriptures, when God spoke, people knew what God had said. It was neither vague nor indiscernible.

Often, a word from God quietly drops into our mind. We might be considering a certain problem when suddenly a fresh idea presents itself. Or when we aren't even thinking about anyone in particular, a name drops into our thoughts. We begin to sense that we should call them or pray for them. God's thoughts are higher than our thoughts, and His ways are superior to ours. If a thought is higher or better than what we would normally think, perhaps it came from God.

We can start with a simple premise. God says we can hear His voice, so when a particularly good thought, idea or solution comes to mind, why not give God credit. After all, we are His creation and He is the one who has given us the ability to think.

A word from God will build us up, encourage us or provide comfort (I Cor. 14:3). God loves us and enjoys strengthening and establishing us, so His words will never tear down or destroy. If even a hint of condemnation exists, the word is not from God. *"Therefore there is now no condemnation for those who are in Christ Jesus,"* (Rom. 8:1). God's thoughts bring freedom, peace, and rest. The Holy Spirit may convict us in an area but always for the purpose of redemption, instruction, warning, correction or restoration, never for condemnation.

God's words, so fresh and alive, often generate an inner response of excitement, a surge of faith, or a sense of peace. A feeling of awe and reverence for God may linger in our hearts. Praise and thankfulness often follow, leading us to worship the Lord.

Know God's Word

How do we, as sheep, get to know His voice so that when a strange voice comes we won't follow it? John 10:4-5 says, *"...and the sheep follow him because they know his voice. And a stranger they simply will not follow, but will flee from him, because they do not know the voice of strangers."*

The answer involves first, a desire to hear and follow God. We must read, study, and familiarize ourselves with the Bible. We need to understand that the secret of recognizing God's voice is connected to knowing His written Word, the "Truth." When we become so familiar with the truth of the Scriptures, if another voice beckons, we immediately recognize it as not coming from God. When we have established ourselves in the Word, then we will more easily recognize truth from error.

You may know that the way the F.B.I. is trained to recognize counterfeit money is not by becoming familiar with counterfeit money. No, they focus on real currency, getting to know it so well that if a counterfeit bill crosses their path, they immediately recognize it. It doesn't match the true, authentic money. The same principle applies to recognizing and identifying spiritual truth.

Other Voices

Recently, I was speaking at a women's retreat on the subject of hearing God's voice. I had been asked to bring two messages. In the first, I talked about hearing a rhema word from the Lord and shared a number of stories. At the break, one of the leaders took me aside and voiced a concern. She was wondering if I planned to talk to the ladies about the importance of aligning a word from God with the Bible. I could tell she was feeling protective of her church women and I appreciated her apprehension.

I was able to ease her mind as I told her that my next message dealt with just that topic, that I shared her concern and would be sure to leave no doubt that we must know the Bible. I assured her that there are guidelines we can follow to test whether a word is from the Lord. My next session went well, and I could see the leader relax as I spoke on the very important topic of discernment.

In truth, there are many voices vying for our attention. Before accepting what we think is a word from God, we need to discern whether God has spoken. Sometimes, we can easily distinguish and other times, the word must be carefully scrutinized and prayed over.

Jesus, when being tempted in the wilderness, discerned the false words of Satan. Satan, who can disguise himself as an angel of light (II Cor. 11:14), spoke to Jesus using Bible verses, but some he twisted and others were partial quotes. Jesus, of course, knew the Word and immediately recognized the error.

Let's look at five voices that originate from sources other than God. With each, we have the freedom to choose whether to listen or not. They include the voice of man, the voice of the world, the voice of error, the voice of deception and the voice of bondage. While our focus is to be on truth, it is good to be aware that voices from each of these groups will make an effort to ensnare our thinking. Let's learn to discern good from evil and move on to maturity. *"But solid food is for the mature, who because of practice have their senses trained to discern good and evil,"* (Heb 5:14).

The Voice of Man

The voice of man, which also refers to our flesh nature, can sometimes fool us into thinking we have heard from God. When we think of the flesh, we think of desires motivated by selfishness, lusts and yearnings that stand apart from godliness. For instance, if we thought we heard a word that we would soon receive a million dollars, a new car or a fur coat, we might want to check the state of our greedy heart. God promises to supply all our needs but not all of our wants. A "name it and claim it" attitude diminishes God and plays on the arrogance of man.

Since the motivating factor in the voice from man's flesh nature is self gratification, it is probably the loudest voice we have to contend with. Our flesh regularly insists on having its way. In order to indulge itself, it may submit to the deeds of the flesh either in thoughts or action. Some are listed in Galatians 5:19-20. *"...immorality, impurity, sensuality, idolatry, sorcery, enmities, strife, jealousy, outbursts of anger, disputes, dissensions, factions, envying, drunkenness, carousing, and things like these...."*

God's voice is different from the voice of our own fleshly desires. Untainted by self centered whims, His voice leads us in ways that build our inner man and prompt us to love, humility and serving others. God's goal is to fashion Christ-like character within us so that we will be spiritually mature and think more of others than ourselves.

When we choose to listen to the voice of God instead of the voice of the flesh, God can renew our minds and build these qualities into our lives: *"...love, joy, peace, patience, kindness, goodness, faithfulness, gentleness, self-control...* (Gal. 5:22-23). We can know by the fruit being produced in our lives whether we are listening to God or to the voice of man.

The Voice of the World

Our next voice is the voice of the world. This voice often asserts itself with many twisted messages. *"For the wisdom of this world is foolishness before God"* (1Co 3:19). As we hold up worldly philosophies to the truth of Scripture, we can quickly see they are not supported in the Bible. These might include issues such as pornography, abortion, euthanasia, homosexuality, adultery, and other personal moral choices. Because the voice of the world is a master when it comes to justifying its ideology and is daily reflected in the media, it is imperative to know the biblical stance on each. The worldly voice has such fine tuned reasoning for its positions that many Christians are drawn into its belief system or at least made to feel without compassion if they refuse to acknowledge and even adhere to its world view. It takes wisdom to sort out all we are confronted with.

A good question to ask in face of world views is, "Will it lead me further into or away from holiness and purity?" God's voice will lead us further into the kingdom of God and His righteousness, not into the kingdom of worldly thought. *"For all that is in the world, the lust of the flesh and the lust of the eyes and the boastful pride of life, is not from the Father, but is from the world"* (I Jn. 2:15-16).

The Voice of Error

Another voice that we might hear is the voice of error. *"We are from God; he who knows God listens to us; he who is not from God does not listen to us. By this we know the spirit of truth and the spirit of error"* (I Jn. 4:6).

Someone once gave me a pamphlet concerning the spirit of truth and the spirit of error. In several columns, it listed various cults and their beliefs. Another column listed what the Bible teaches concerning each issue. The erroneous teachings of one cult said that there was no atoning value in Jesus' death. Another stated that one sacrifice was insufficient to pay the debt of sin. On the truth side were several Bible verses stating that the blood of Jesus cleanses us from all sin.

A common error holds to the belief that we must work our way to heaven, that salvation is by good works. Many well meaning people, caught in this false teaching, miss out on the true grace of God. The Bible clearly teaches that, while works should follow salvation, salvation itself is *"...by grace through faith and not of works..."* (Eph.2:8-9). Yet, many adhere to this voice of error.

On a recent trip to Florida, I engaged in a conversation with a man from India who practiced the Hindu faith. I asked him a question. "How do Hindu's deal with sin?" He basically explained that by doing good deeds, they counter balanced any sin they commit. I wondered how many good deeds he would have to perform to be good enough or if it was endless.

Held against Christianity, the error was obvious. The spirit of error always questions and challenges the simple truths of the Bible, especially when it comes to the finished work of Christ on the cross.

I shared with him that my faith offered a different solution. Jesus, by shedding His blood on the cross, had atoned for all my sin. Because of that, I could know, not only that my sins were forgiven, but that I would have eternal life with God. Of course, he had many gods to pacify. I wondered if he ever felt truly free.

Many religions and cults exist in the world today, advocating half-truths that sound appealing. The Bible teaches that only Christianity is pure truth. *"All Scripture is inspired by God and profitable for teaching, for reproof, for correction, for training in righteousness"* (II Tim. 3:16). Other religions, though they may adopt some truth, base many of their fundamental tenets on error. People, caught in the web of these inaccurate belief systems, mistakenly think they have heard from God. As a result, they establish their whole lives on error.

It is interesting to note that many people today consider themselves spiritual. But what does that really mean? New Age? Buddhist? Astrology? Tarot cards? Black Magic? Scientology? There are many ideas and religious systems that come under the topic of "spiritual." Some embrace obvious error, while others are more subtle. Don't be fooled. A number of false teachings are touted as "spiritual" today.

For example, if we hear a voice of new age philosophy telling us to buy a crystal for good luck or to look to the stars or horoscopes for direction, we must discern that the voice of error has spoken. Deuteronomy 18:9-11 is a good section to reference.

As Christians, we trust in Jesus. He alone is our Lord and thereby allotted full control of what comes into our lives. It is an insult to His integrity to call Jesus, "Lord," yet look for direction from another source. How perilous to allow another god to determine our fate.

Scripture gives clear warning about being alert to the voice of error. *"For if he who comes preaches another Jesus whom we have not preached, or if you receive a different spirit which you have not received, or a different gospel which you have not accepted--you may well put up with it!"* (II Cor. 11:4 NKJV)

In other words, beware of false teaching and disqualify it for what it is. God's voice will always lead us to truth. His voice lines up with

His written Word. It will not lead to confusion, as error often does, but will lead to order, fulfillment, and most of all, truth.

The Voice of Deception

Closely aligned with the voice of error is the voice of deception. These two voices often mesh together and are capable of causing much confusion as they entangle hearts with their trickery. We can know the voice of deception because it will represent itself as truth, while all the time knowing it is false. Its motive is to mislead and cause people to follow the wrong course. Deception is a form of lying. Frequently, when faced with deception, we will sense that something is not quite right. We may not be able to put our finger on exactly what it is, but we sense we are in a "red flag" situation.

A friend of mine moved away from sound teaching. Subscribing to ideas that appealed to her, she convinced me I would enjoy reading them as well. As I read, I felt uncomfortable but wasn't sure why, so I asked Bill to review them to see if he could discern what troubled me. He immediately saw the deceptive error. All of the teachings encouraged believers away from any authority in their lives. They ignored such verses as 1Corinthians 11:3, *"But I want you to understand that Christ is the head of every man, and the man is the head of a woman, and God is the head of Christ."* Instead, they encouraged an independent attitude which, of course, is not a biblical concept.

We must be sensitive to the Holy Spirit to avoid the error of deception. Jim Jones and other false teachers have expounded on visions which sounded plausible, but their deception eventually left many with shattered lives and, in some cases, death.

"But the Spirit explicitly says that in later times some will fall away from the faith, paying attention to deceitful spirits and doctrines of demons" (I Tim. 4:1). Timothy indicates that we have a choice whether to pay attention to deception, strong though it may be.

Deception comes in many forms. Sometimes, voices people listen to tell them to make excuses for their behavior. Sometimes, deception convinces a person that they are powerless in a bad situation. Satan, the father of lies, glories in defrauding people with a voice of hopelessness or a voice of shame. While deception can be rooted in disappointment, the Bible reveals that God has given us power, provided hope and carried our shame to the cross. He has given many wonderful promises which we can claim. For every lie, there is a truth that counteracts.

Lies hold us captive. Truth sets us free. God's voice is perfect truth. There is no deceit in Him. He speaks only those things that are blameless and upright.

The Voice of Bondage

We should be aware that the path of the voice of deception is often an attempt to lead us into bondage or slavery. *"For you have not received a spirit of slavery leading to fear again..."* (Rom. 8:15). At one time, we were all bound to sin, but when we accepted Christ as Lord and Savior, He freed us from the bondage and penalty of sin and released us from death. If we heed the voice of bondage, however, it has the power to enslave us with fear.

A speaker came to our town one year and taught the women who attended his meetings that they could not hope to be godly unless they changed their ways. (Notice his works theology in what followed). His words were full of authority and control as he manipulated the women, influencing them into decisions that were biblically unnecessary. His assertions included such commands as these: Women must wear skirts at all times, never slacks. Earrings and other jewelry must be cast aside and placed in the basket being passed around. They are not pleasing to the Lord. To the list of "don'ts," he also added that holidays must not be celebrated. They were of the devil. His words were compelling, mesmerizing, and sounded credible to many of the women. They were convinced and gripped by his persuasive speech.

My guess is that, right now, you can see through the bondage he was placing the women under. His words were not those of freedom;

they were words of law. No grace was offered, just a list of rules to follow. Do you see the works theology and the bondage it introduced?

Sometimes, as I suspect in this case, leaders influence and persuade people to follow their own convictions or personal desires. In his case, instead of trusting God, he set himself up as the authority and took a position of control. It became legalism and bondage when he thrust his personal opinion, albeit his misguided viewpoint about women, onto his audience, compelling them to follow his mandates. In a perverted way, he tried to play the role of the Holy Spirit in their lives. Unfortunately, his ill-advised perspective had the potential to ensnare and enslave others. Bondage is a serious issue that can shut a person down.

When this preacher finished, some of these vulnerable women, sadly, had accepted the yoke of bondage and fear. As they listened, they internalized every word as though he represented God's voice. Later, when one woman spoke to me about the meeting, her remark said it all, "I felt so condemned, so bad about myself." Perhaps, that should have been a hint that his message was amiss.

God's voice brings freedom and peace. It promotes true inner godliness. Again, Romans 8:1 cannot be stressed enough as a reminder, *"Therefore there is now no condemnation for those who are in Christ Jesus."* Feeling condemned is an indicator that we have left the truth of Scripture.

The voice of bondage usually focuses on the outer man, that is, things we "should be doing" to prove we are holy. God looks at the inner person (I Sam. 16:7). Holiness is a heart issue, not a works issue. Jesus said that the truth would set us free, not lead to an oppressive fear and condemnation.

"All things are lawful for me, but not all things are profitable. All things are lawful for me, but I will not be mastered by anything" (I Cor. 6:12). We are not under the law but have a higher calling to be led by the Holy Spirit. We don't need to be bound by any man's personal laws. If God wants something changed in our lives, the Holy Spirit can and often will personally convict us. Romans 14 is good reading on this subject.

From our look at five voices that vie for our attention, the voice of man, the voice of the world, the voice of error, the voice of deception and the voice of bondage, we see there is a need to test the voices and the spirits behind them to be sure what we are hearing has originated with God. Let's look at the topic of testing the spirits next.

Test the Spirits

Is it possible for a believer to think he has heard from God when actually he has not? Yes, it is. I John 4:1 exhorts us in this way, *"Beloved, do not believe every spirit, but test the spirits to see whether they are from God; because many false prophets have gone out into the world."*

In Matthew 24:4, Jesus confirms that we need to be cautious when He says, *"...See to it that no one misleads you."* Colossians 2:8 agrees with these words, *"See to it that no one takes you captive through philosophy and empty deception, according to the tradition of men, according to the elementary principles of the world, rather than according to Christ."* Surely, we need to be discerning and alert.

Let's look at some people in the Bible who fell into the trap of believing other voices without testing the spirit behind them. As outsiders, it is easy for us to see their error. Perhaps, we can learn from their mistakes.

Adam and Eve

Adam and Eve would have done well to have tested the spirits. In contemplating their situation, we can learn how to avoid similar problems in our own lives. Genesis 3 tells us that the serpent was more crafty than any beast. The word crafty means deceptive which means Eve had an encounter with the voice of deception. Her first mistake came when she listened to a voice that clearly opposed what God had already told her. God had said she would die if she ate from the tree of the knowledge of good and evil. The voice of deception questioned the truth of God's proclamation. The serpent gave reasons why the fruit should be eaten. You may have noticed in life that deception always justifies itself. It often conceals truth by use of reasoning that sounds logical and pleasing. Listening to the voice of deception, Eve made her decision to partake of the fruit.

Then Adam came along, and he listened to another voice. Without any thought about what God had said, Adam saw his wife eat and decided it must be okay for him, too. He responded to the voice of man, his own fleshly desire.

Unfortunately, responding to other voices left them both in a state of broken fellowship with God as the first sin entered the world. Listening to the voice of deception and the voice of the flesh actually built a wall between them and God.

Ananias and Saphira

Instead of testing the spirits, Ananias and Saphira put the Spirit of the Lord to the test in Acts 5:9. They kept back a portion of the price they received for the sale of some property. First, they listened to the voice of deception by planning to keep some of the money they had promised to others. Then, they listened to the voice of the flesh by lying. Peter questioned Ananias, "...*Why has Satan filled your heart to lie to the Holy Spirit*" (Acts 5:3)? That was an interesting question in that it defined who was behind the deception and lying, none other than Satan, the father of lies (Jn. 8: 44).

Had Ananias and Saphira considered the voice of God, they would have known that lying and deception defy God's Word and character. But they didn't test the spirits and thereby put God's Holy Spirit to the test.

Staying close to the written Word helps us to know when God is speaking. We want to learn to detect His voice so that when other voices, the flesh, the world, error, deception and bondage come along, they will be easily discerned. When we feel attracted by their persuasiveness, a caution light will go on in our mind, and we won't be fooled or tricked. Grounded in the Word, we stand strong.

Once we establish that we have heard God's voice, we need to take the next step of faith. God wants us to cooperate with the things He reveals to us. In our next chapter, we will explore obedience. I know...that word, obedience, can have negative connotations. You may be surprised, then, at the approach we will take.

Study Guide 9

1. Name the four guidelines used to check the validity of a word.
    Explain each.
    A.

    B.

    C.

    D.

2. Share an experience when these guidelines lined up for you.

3. If one of the guidelines fails to line up, why is it prudent to wait?

4. Give an example when a word was clearly from God.

5. A. Why is it important to be committed to a church?

    B. What guidelines help us know whether our needs are being met in a church?

6. Describe ways to recognize God's voice.

7. What caution can we apply from Peter's fishing experience in Luke 5:5-7?

8. A. In thinking of John 10:4-5, why is it essential to know God's word?
    B. What is the secret to recognizing a strange voice?

9. Write a short description of each of the following:
    A. Voice of man - I Corinthians 2:11, Galatians 5:19-20

    B. Voice of the world - I Corinthians 2:12, I John 2:15-16

C. Voice of error - I John 4:6

D. Voice of deception - I Timothy 4:1,3

E. Voice of bondage - Romans 8:15, Romans 14

10. How would these people have benefited from testing the spirits (I John 4:1)?

    A. Adam and Eve - Genesis 3

    B. Ananias and Saphira - Acts 5

CHAPTER 10

Blessing "Under the Umbrella"

"I delight to do Your will, O my God;
Your Law is within my heart" (Ps. 40:8).

The Importance of the Umbrella

A S A FATHER, Bill would sometimes take walks with our children on rainy days. In their excitement, the girls would occasionally slip out from the covering of the umbrella. Immediately hit by the pelting rain, cold and wet, they would slip back under the umbrella where they were safe and dry.

I think the same thing can happen to us in a spiritual sense. In God's economy, the place of safety, prosperity, and blessing can be found "under the umbrella" of His protection. Under His covering, instruction and direction, we can rest as we follow His lead. It is the place where we, as believers, find our greatest fulfillment, satisfaction and purpose in life.

Think about this prayer and see if you find it as intriguing as I do. *Lord, let's do something together that requires my obedience and your faithfulness and will result in mutual delight.* Doesn't that sound appealing, like an adventure with God? His part and ours, coming together with a result of delight, enjoyment, and pleasure for both of us. I wonder if this might be a new way to look at following God's promptings, one with an expectation of cooperating with God with an end goal of shared enjoyment.

Kathryn Kuhlman once said, "If you're going to be led by the Holy Spirit, you have to be willing to follow." If we can retune our minds to consider that obedience might actually be a good thing, a pleasurable thing, would that make a difference?

God cares so much about each one of us that He longs for us to experience His love, peace, and joy to the fullest. His plans for our lives are the best possible. Believers often lament that they want to be full of the Holy Spirit and walk close to God but sometimes forget an important principle. Growing fruit in our lives depends on our willingness to come "under the umbrella" of God's protection and authority.

In John 15:10-11, a secret about obedience is revealed. A promise is given that when we choose to comply, we are in position to receive fullness of joy. *"If you keep My commandments, you will abide in My love.... These things I have spoken to you, that My joy may be in you, and that your joy may be made full."* Notice the "if, then" aspect of God's offer. We keep His commandments, and then we get to abide in His love and enjoy the wonderful gift of fullness of joy.

At this point, you may be asking yourself: What does all this have to do with hearing God's voice? My answer would be: Basically, everything. Here's why. Suppose you hear a word from God giving you specific direction in your life. You have held the word up to biblical principles, prayed about it, felt at peace, and even sought the counsel of a godly friend. You now have a choice to make. Will you do what God has asked, or will you just savor the possibility and choose not to? If it is truly God speaking to you, then isn't it important to respond to what He has asked? Granted, God won't run you under the bus if you choose not to follow His lead, but think about the joy and the blessing you may miss.

If I had not obeyed when God asked me to go to Europe, I would have missed out on the trip of a lifetime along with special ministry opportunities (Chapter 7). If I had not heeded God's voice and had opted to stay home from my class reunion, I would have forfeited a personal healing in my heart (Chapter 3). If I had not listened to God's voice to persist in seeking Mike's college scholarship, believing that nothing was impossible with God, Mike might have accumulated unnecessary college debt (Chapter 4).

Sadly, I have watched people get a clear word from God, one that resonates with the Word and with everyone they know, but then fail to move forward with it. Some of these people had grand dreams of ministry, evangelism, going on the mission field, writing books, but never made the choice to step out in faith. While pondering an idea and mulling it over is pleasurable, it is not the same as stepping out in faith and moving forward with a plan. No doubt, we can all look back at possible missed blessings, but the good news is that we can start fresh right now and choose to cooperate with God's plans from this point on. We can know that God is trustworthy because Job 23:14 says, *"For He performs what is appointed for me, and many such decrees are with Him."* It's exciting to know that God has many future plans prepared for us to walk in. Let's jump on board!

Receiving a word from God is a wonderful opportunity for us to partner with Him in a great adventure of faith. Bill had an opportunity some years ago to trust God in a very hard situation, one that took him far out of his comfort zone, far from his perceived ability for handling a situation. It started with a phone call from a friend informing him that a family in our church had just taken their child to the hospital. Unbelievably, the toddler had been run over by a large earthmoving bulldozer and was in critical condition.

Not only were the couples extended family out of town, but both of our pastors were, too. It was a frightening and incredibly emotional situation. *What can I do to help?* Bill thought. By faith, he drove to the hospital where the child had been taken by ambulance in hopes of saving his life. But it was too late. The child went to be with the Lord. Bill felt both terrified and inadequate to be of help in this situation. But deciding to stay "under the umbrella," God gave him strength to minister to the family with compassion, tenderness and support that went beyond his understanding. Today, this family still warmly speaks with gratitude for the comfort and care Bill provided for them that day.

There are times like this when we have to make a quick decision whether to follow God's lead or not. If Bill had drawn back, he would have missed an important opportunity to serve and the blessing of knowing God's presence in a profoundly difficult situation. It was "under the umbrella" that Bill and the family experienced God's grace and power. It is "under the umbrella" that we experience the fullness of God's calling in our lives. As we listen to God's voice, there is almost always a call to follow and trust. This is what living a life of faith is all about.

Christianity is not just another religion. It is a very personal relationship with Jesus Christ. Jesus, the living Lord, is the One who interacts with people, speaks to them, calls them forth, and tasks them with important requests regarding themselves or others. These requests require an answer, one that prompts us to faith and leads us to action. Four times in scripture, we are told, *"The righteous shall live by faith,* (Hab. 2:4, Gal. 3:11, and Phil. 3:9, Rom. 1:17). As we live by faith, the result is blessing. If we sense the Holy Spirit nudging us, we must choose to open our hearts. So, when He calls, let's confidently respond by faith and let the adventure begin.

The Dress

For several days, as I entered my prayer time, the name of a particular friend came to mind. As I prayed for her, God impressed on me that she needed money. Forty dollars came to mind. I sensed it would be used to buy an item of clothing.

Often, when we receive a word from God, our mind attempts to apply logic. We try to rationalize whether the word seems reasonable. At first, the thought of giving her money seemed ridiculous. What would she think? It might embarrass both of us. I'm imagining things. Surely they have enough money.

I share these thoughts because they are not atypical when listening for God's voice. Remember, the enemy wants to thwart God's plans and make His words appear strange or outlandish. Satan's job description includes killing, stealing, and destroying (Jn. 10:10). He delights in frustrating and preventing the completion of God's work on every level. His mission is to hinder and oppose anything that might bring blessing.

After several days of contemplating the prompting of the Holy Spirit, I decided to step out in faith. As a gentleman, the Holy Spirit never forces us into anything against our will, but instead, He gently nudges, prompts and encourages us.

I asked Bill what he thought about me giving my friend the money. He released me to do what I felt God wanted. This was a situation where it was good to solicit "confirmation from others." I asked Bill, since, as my husband, he is my earthly "umbrella." With his go-ahead, I wrote out a check for forty dollars, slipped it into an envelope and had Kim deliver it to their door when she went out to run errands.

Because we were leaving for vacation that day, I didn't hear the end of the story until the next week. It seemed that, for several weeks, my friend had admired a special dress at a local store but knew she didn't have enough money to buy it. Each day as she drove past the store, she looked for the dress in the window. Then, she began to pray that if the Lord wanted her to have it, He would provide the money and save that particular dress for her.

Delighted to receive the forty dollars, she had rushed to the store during her lunch hour, only to find it closed. They were marking clothes down for a sale. Feeling frustrated that by the time she would get there the next day, things would be picked over, she prayed and decided to trust God.

At noon the following day, she scurried to the store. To her delight, she found the dress still on the rack. Quickly, she found the size. It was a ten, just her size. For the sale, they had marked it down to forty-three dollars, half price. Excited by God's provision, she joyfully purchased the dress.

Later, she shared with me that God had also given her a verse of encouragement from the Psalms. *"Delight yourself in the Lord; and He will give you the desires of your heart"* (Ps. 37:4). We both felt blessed by what the Lord had done. Hearing God's voice and acting on it had proved a source of encouragement and fulfillment for both of us. It was definitely an occasion when obedience met God's faithfulness and resulted in mutual delight.

A Nudge from God

Rod, a friend of Bill's shared this powerful story. A woman in his church sensed God prompting her to invite an acquaintance to church. She didn't follow up right away and call her, and even when she saw her in a local store, she dismissed the thought. Twice more on the same day, she ran into her in the store, and although this was the first time she had seen her in years, she finally decided to step out and invite her to church.

The next day, Sunday, she was pleased to see the woman actually followed through and came. But that's not the end of the story. After the service, the invited woman told her that the reason she had been at the store the day before was to buy food for a nice dinner for her family, after which she had planned to end her life.

Because of a little nudge from an old acquaintance inviting her to come to church, the woman had changed her mind about taking her life and came to church instead. A little nudge, yes, but I would guess the woman who had the nudge listens even more carefully today. Imagine if she hadn't.

Laziness

Sometimes, we hear God asking us to do something, and we come up with one excuse or another as to why we can't or don't want to do it. We're too busy, maybe tomorrow, or we don't feel like it right now. For me, one time was just laziness.

Several years ago, I experienced a time when God had spoken many things for me to do. I had chosen not to do any of them. My excuses varied: I've got too much to do today. I don't feel like it. I'll do it tomorrow. It doesn't matter if I don't do this. It doesn't sound fun. It makes me uncomfortable. On and on my excuses went until one day they all caught up with me, and I suddenly realized that I felt far away from God.

"What can I do?" I lamented to Bill. "I've neglected to listen to God's voice in so many things that now I don't know where to start. How will I ever get right with the Lord again? I feel so depressed about the whole thing."

With wisdom and understanding, Bill counseled me toward a simple solution to a problem that seemed complex and overwhelming to me. "Betsy, why don't you just ask God to forgive you for not obeying, then ask Him to wipe the slate clean? Make an appeal for a fresh start. Ask Him to give you just one area to comply with today, and tell Him you are willing to listen to Him seriously from now on."

Sometimes, we simply need to go to God and come back "under the umbrella." After all, He is still holding it, just waiting for our return with love and grace.

What relief I felt just having a plan. Eagerly, I went to God in prayer. Graciously, he poured out His mercy and forgiveness and restored His presence to me. He gave me one person to call that day, and this time I followed through. It felt good to be back under the umbrella.

Fear

Sometimes, we find ourselves caught up in fear that paralyzes us from moving out in submission to God's requests. Fear of the unknown can be difficult to overcome. We don't always know what will result from heeding God's voice, and it can seem threatening to move into action without knowing what might happen. What if the situation ends badly, we think.

The Israelites, after crossing the Jordon River, were poised to enter the Promised Land, but spies who were sent out came back with this challenge, "There are giants in the land!" With these words, fear spread throughout the Jewish tribes.

All but two of the spies, Joshua and Caleb, feared what might come about if they went into the land. God's purpose was for them to go forward and claim the land He had given them but fear ultimately stopped them. As a result, the people forfeited many blessings because of their disobedience. Their wandering in the desert continued for forty years simply because they had allowed their fear to overtake them with rebellion against God's desire for them. They missed out on God's best plan. They stepped out from "under the umbrella". Sadly, that entire generation died in the wilderness, never seeing the land God had promised. Only two people made it in, the two spies who had believed God. The rest only saw a potentially bad situation. They left God out of the equation.

There are times when the Lord also asks us to do something and, immediately, fear wells up in our heart. *I can't do that, Lord. I'm too afraid.* If we have heard from God, we need to come to the point where we don't want to miss the blessing on the other side, where the thought of blessing supersedes our apprehension.

One way to overcome fear is to look at God's direction as an opportunity for adventure. It is exciting to observe and be part of the unfolding of an exploit. Just as light overcomes darkness, so faith overcomes fear. As dread diminishes, faith grows and becomes bigger than our anxiety.

Faith in God's love for us is the answer to fear. *"...Perfect love casts out fear..."* (I Jn. 4:18). As we understand how much God loves us, we begin to trust that he will only lead us into things that are good for us, sometimes hard, but always good. To do otherwise would go against His character.

We can also know that God never asks us to do something without going ahead of us. He initiates, and leads and we follow. Once we begin to see that God is faithful, we can look forward to the adventures He has for us.

Mall Janitor

I had an unusual meeting with fear on a shopping trip. As I drove to the mall to do some shopping one morning, I spent the hour drive singing worship songs and praying. Feeling close to God, I committed my day to Him with these words, *Lord, do whatever you want with my life today. I submit myself to you, and I'm willing to go wherever you lead and do whatever you want.* Little did I know where this prayer would take me that day.

Upon arriving at the mall, my first stop was the ladies restroom. On the way out, I caught a glimpse of a cleaning lady. As I walked back into the store, a thought whispered in my mind, *Go talk to the cleaning lady.*

What? I don't even know her.

Go talk to the cleaning lady, my mind persisted.

This is ridiculous! What in the world would I say to her? It's crazy! I could feel fear rising up in my heart.

Just tell her I love her, came the gentle voice.

By this time, all concentration on shopping had left, and my mind was totally focused on a cleaning lady I had never seen or met before. Wrestling with my thoughts for about ten minutes, I struggled between fear and faith. Thankfully, faith won. *Ok, Lord, this better be from you. Here I go.*

Back to the restroom I went, heart pounding loudly, hands wet from nervous perspiration. The restroom was full of people as I sat down in a chair in the ante room outside the restroom where the cleaning lady had left her bucket. No one was in that area. *Lord, if this is really from you, confirm it to me by having the cleaning lady come out here by herself.* No sooner had I whispered that prayer than the entire restroom cleared of people and the cleaning lady appeared, mop in hand.

Sheepishly approaching her and feeling ludicrous, I said, "This may seem kind of strange to you," (at which she stepped back from me, not knowing what to expect), "but the Lord has given me a word for you." I pressed on. "He wants you to know that He loves you. He sees the situations you are facing in your life, and He has a plan for you. He cares about everything you are going through."

She paused a moment. I held my breath. A tear came to her eye as she looked me square in the face. "Thank you so much for telling me that," she said with much emotion. "You don't know how much I needed to hear that today."

We said little more and I left, relieved to do my shopping, knowing that for a brief moment the cleaning lady and I had touched God together. I had put my fear aside and allowed God to use me to bring a special message to a troubled soul. It seemed a foolish thing to do, was totally out of character for me, and rendered me in a state of anxiety. Yet God did something special and unforgettable in that encounter. I discovered that it pays to obey even when the assignment seems eccentric and fearful. "Under the umbrella," God can accomplish powerful exploits. God and I had partnered for an adventure together.

Angry Customer

While one side of fear may come from knowing what to do and feeling uneasy about doing it, the other side of fear lies in not knowing what God wants us to do. There are times we really sense a need in a situation and want to know what direction to go, but God is quiet on the matter. We may become anxious and uneasy because we don't have a clear word. An ancient, unknown author speaks well to this situation, *"Never act in panic nor allow men to dictate to thee; calm thyself and be still; force thyself into the quiet of thy closet until the pulse beats normally and the scare has ceased to disturb. When thou art most eager to act is the time when thou wilt make the pitiable mistakes. Do not say in thine heart what thou wilt or wilt not do, but wait upon God until He makes known His way. So long as that way is hidden, it is clear that there is no need of action, and that He accounts Himself responsible for all the results of keeping thee where thou art."*

In modern English, I think the author is simply trying to encourage the reader to refrain from acting when we are in a state of panic. Until our heart is calm, it is prudent to wait. Then, until God reveals a plan to move forward, we can know that He is responsible for us while we are in waiting mode.

Bill had an encounter at one point in his career where God used an interesting chain of events to dismantle a tricky situation, one that involved waiting on the Lord. For many years, Bill worked in sales, calling on major companies in his region. Occasionally, he dealt with an unhappy customer. Often, these people were surly about life in general. On one such occasion, a scowling buyer greeted him. Upset and angry, he had nothing pleasant to say about Bill, his company or their products. Although Bill had done nothing wrong, the buyer's self sustaining wrath only grew as he heard his own words. Finally, he ended an hour long tirade with a cold command.

"I'm going out to lunch, and I want you to be here when I return. I'm not finished yet!" he exploded.

Shaken, Bill found a phone to confirm a lunch date with a Christian friend. He looked forward to having his wounds soothed and his soul comforted. Reaching his friend by phone, he wasn't prepared to hear, "Gee, Bill, I'm sorry, but I can't make it today after all." Somewhat unnerved and feeling abandoned, Bill wondered why God had allowed the cancellation of his lunch date at a time when he needed a friend the most. Upset and not really hungry, he decided to just sit in his car and read Scripture until it was time to face the buyer again. Perhaps, the Lord would give some direction or comfort before he had to return.

Not sure where to turn, Bill simply opened his Bible at random. It fell open to Proverbs, where his eyes were drawn to chapter 15, verse 1, *"A gentle answer turns away wrath, but a harsh word stirs up anger."* Bill's response was interesting. At first, these words calmed him, but as he read the rest of the chapter, it was like God gave him a "heart implant" of love and compassion for the buyer. After a time of prayer, Bill felt prepared to meet again with his normally friendly, but now, upset buyer.

This time, Bill was equipped and ready to heed God's council. For every accusation spouted by the buyer, Bill confidently, yet gently, gave a reply. At first, the man raved on but then something changed. With each composed answer from Bill, the man calmed a bit. Within five minutes, the buyer collected himself and even apologized. Bill sensed the awesome presence of God in the situation with his every response. Confident, quiet, Spirit filled words had melted this gruff, brash man. Bill's straightforward compliance with God's plan was rewarded.

Where did Bill's confidence and strength come from? Clearly, coming "under the umbrella" of God's protection during his lunch break had made all the difference. God had spoken direction for reconciliation through the Scriptures. Bill had received a rhema word, acted on it and seen the fruit. It is so important to remember that when God sends forth His word, it contains the power to perform and accomplish its purposes. Clearly, by cooperating with God's purpose, Bill experienced a good outcome.

What was the result for Bill? *"So faith comes from hearing and hearing by the word of Christ"* (Rom.10:17). Bill had heard a word from the Lord and as a result, his faith soared. God had redeemed a thorny situation through the word He spoke to him.

Two Encounters at the Grocery Store

While some words of direction from God may be met with fear, not every word will be. There are many times when we just move forward almost without a second thought. I recall one time when I was in the grocery store, and I noticed a middle aged, heavy-set woman grimacing in pain as she held onto the meat counter for support. Immediately, I felt a nudge that I should offer to pray with her. I approached her without even taking time to consider my own fear. She was happy to receive prayer for her unsteady, painful legs. After a simple prayer, we separated ways. Later, I smiled as I saw her walking with ease down one of the aisles. Not every word from God has to be contemplated and chewed on, considered and reconsidered.

With some nudges from God, like that one, we just go into automatic pilot. Our pastor once said these words of wisdom, "Compassion really isn't compassion unless we act on it."

Another grocery store encounter occurred as I was driving my car into a choice parking space at our local Kroger's store. As I pulled in, I caught a glimpse of another car coming up the lane from the opposite direction. She stopped her car, and with a defiant, angry look on her face yelled out the window, "That's my parking place!"

I have never been yelled at in this way and was curious as to what had her so riled up. Just before I leaned out my window to answer her, I felt the Lord tap my shoulder to respond with calmness and sincere kindness, so I smiled and said, "Oh, I'm so sorry, I will be happy to move and let you park here." With that, I backed out and found another parking space.

But, there's more to the story. As I busied myself at the vegetable counter in the store, I noticed the woman from the parking lot maneuvering toward me. She was in a wheelchair. I was stunned because I had not realized she was handicapped when we had our parking lot encounter. It had not been a handicapped spot we were vying for. I quickly thanked God that He had encouraged me to give a kind response to this poor soul. As she wheeled up to me, I could tell she wanted to say something. Her words were so heartfelt, I wanted to hug her as she explained, "Thank you so much for giving me the parking space. I can't tell you how many times I'm almost there and someone pulls in front of me. It's so aggravating. I want to apologize for my rudeness to you."

Of course, I accepted her apology and felt God had taught me a very careful lesson not to harden my heart when others act in an unkind manner. Instead, he wants me to respond gently and with grace, even when they are out of sorts. We never know what they may be dealing with. A wise teacher once taught me that we have a choice as to how we respond to people. We can look at them through our own eyes and at times, be disgruntled, or we can look at them through Jesus' eyes. In which case, we can then reflect to others the heart of Jesus. Of course, that would be grace, kindness, and understanding.

The Shoes

One more story about responding to the prompting of the Holy Spirit involved a shoe order I had placed. Needing some new shoes, I decided to order a pair through a company I had done business with before. When the shoes arrived, I realized they didn't fit right. I mailed them back and selected another pair. To my dismay, the second pair didn't fit either.

What should I do? As I prayed, the Lord dropped a name into my mind and said, *Why don't you order a pair of shoes for Donna instead?* Toying with the thought, I sighed, thinking perhaps that would be a good idea.

Catalog in hand, I invited Donna for a visit to see if I had correctly discerned the Lord's voice. As I explained how God seemed to be directing me to offer her a new pair of shoes, she burst out crying. "Betsy, I have desperately needed shoes. I've been pleading with the Lord to provide a pair. In fact, this need has been at the top of my prayer list. I can't thank you enough for listening to the Lord and offering to meet my need for shoes." From Donna's response, I'm convinced God spoke to me to order her the much needed shoes in exchange for the shoes I had ordered for myself.

Whether it's a fresh word or meeting a need, we are to be God's vessels of compassion. An adventure awaits each one of us as we choose to be "under the umbrella" and partake of the blessings God has for us. God's desire is for our growth and fruitfulness. He wants to use us as vessels to carry His love and His message. This includes listening to His voice and heeding His word. This is the place of abundant living, full of purpose and meaning.

Final Thoughts

"You have seen today that God speaks to man" (Deut. 5:24).

Throughout this book, we have seen that God speaks to people. He does so in many and varied ways, through Scripture, during prayer, in circumstances, through people, in visions and dreams, and through His marvelous creation. Many times, His Word comes through our thoughts. Even the writing of this book came as a result of God speaking to me long ago to journal stories depicting my relationship with Him. Over the course of many years, I recorded life events where I discerned God was interacting with me. On a number of occasions, I read and reread what I had written, trying to find some sort of a common thread that tied the stories together. I labored, pondered and revisited my stories frequently but could not discern a common thread.

Then one day, a prophetic teacher from England, Norman Barnes, visited our church. After he gave his message, he began to call out people in the congregation to impart a word from God to specific individuals. I was one he called. As he prayed over me and prophesied, he said there was something on the back burner of my life that God was bringing up to the front burner. I knew immediately that he was speaking of my writing. His word resonated with me as a rhema word.

The next day I got out my journals once again, and as I had so many times before, I looked over my stories, trying to determine some kind of cohesive pattern. This time, almost immediately, I saw it. All of my stories fit into a package of God speaking to me. Over the years, He had spoken to me in many ways, and I saw that each story fit into a particular heading which eventually formed a chapter. In the end, I had established ten chapters, which together illustrated the faithfulness of God as He had spoken to my heart in many ways over the years. Bill, and a few friends, also added stories to round out some of the chapters.

I believe every Christian, who is walking with the Lord, longs to hear God's voice. Surely, our larger destiny in life is built from a compilation of smaller events and experiences, many of which are directly connected with a whisper from the heart of God. It's all about God expanding us, rearranging us, building us, setting a course for us, thrilling us, delighting us, and blessing us so that we are positioned with strength to serve others, disciple others, and compassionately love others. In the end, it's all about Him.

Beyond the obvious responses that God desires when He imparts a rhema word to us, we must remember the exhortation given in Hebrews 13:15-16, *"Through Him then, let us continually offer up a sacrifice of praise to God, that is, the fruit of lips that give thanks to His name. And do not neglect doing good and sharing; for with such sacrifices God is pleased."*

God is interested in developing in us a heart attitude of thanksgiving. When we experience the refreshing blessings in store for us as we choose to come "under the umbrella" and listen to His voice, our response can't help but be one of thankfulness. So, speak to us, Lord. We're listening.

Study Guide 10

1. Discuss Kathryn Kuhlman's statement, "If you're going to be led by the Holy Spirit, you have to be willing to follow."

2. What is meant by the term "under the umbrella"?

3. Share a time when you knew you were in that position?

4. A. Comment on the saying, *Impression without expression causes depression* in light of obedience.

    B. Have you experienced a time when you realized you had not responded to God's voice? How did you handle it?

5. Name some hindrances to hearing God's voice.

6. Share a blessing that you have experienced from obedience to a word from God.

7. A. What does this statement mean to you? *Lord, let's do something together that requires my obedience and your faithfulness and will result in mutual delight.*

    B. Are you ready to pray this as your prayer?

8. Explain the following verses:
    A. Ps.119:114 *"You are my hiding place and my shield; I wait for Your <u>word.</u>"*
    B. Job 23:12b *"I have treasured the <u>words</u> of His mouth more than my necessary food."*
    C. Deut. 13:14 *"...<u>Listen to His voice</u>, serve Him, and cling to Him."*

Acknowledgments

M Y FIRST ACKNOWLEDGEMENT is a huge thank you to Jesus Christ, my Lord and Savior. You have guided me through this project, filling me with joy and thankfulness. I praise you for the wonderful God you are and for the opportunity to serve you through writing. May your Name be blessed and exalted. You are worthy of all praise.

This book has been a labor of love for several people. I appreciate the hours of editing and support the following people gave me.

Bill, my faithful husband, you are a rock in my life, an anchor who keeps me on track. I am so thankful for your words of wisdom, for keeping me sensitive and realistic, and for the hours you spent going over each chapter. Your input in editing content has been so important to me and your insights of great value, even when you have felt chapters needed radical change. Thank you for your honest assessments, and your help, freely given. I always felt encouraged.

Kim, my beloved daughter, you have been such a dear to take time, when your discretionary time is so limited, to edit my book for flow. Sometimes, chapters came back completely rearranged but always made so much more sense when you were finished. You are an example of a godly woman who gives of herself and her gifts to be of assistance wherever you can. I am so grateful to you for your wisdom, your clarity of thought, and your love. It has all been significant.

Sue, my dear friend, what would I have done without your expertise in punctuation? Your hours spent meticulously reviewing each sentence are so appreciated. I have learned a lot from you. Your continual encouragement and support have inspired and cheered me.

To all my readers, I am blessed and humbled that you are taking time to read my book. My prayer is that you will grow closer to God and that you will be more aware that He does speak to you, maybe more often than you imagined.

Another Title by Betsy Tacchella: "Mother Has Alzheimer's," a book dealing with hope in the midst of any loss, can be purchased at Amazon.com or Barnes and Noble. Please visit the author's website and blog at www.betsytacchella.com.